DANCING
WITH
YESTERDAY'S SHADOWS

When Where You've Been is Keeping You from Where You Want to Go

David G. Beighley, Ph.D.

GOSPEL FILMS™
PUBLICATIONS

©Gospel Films, Inc. Box 455; Muskegon, MI 49443-0455
616-773-3361 Toll Free: 1-800-253-0413 Fax: 616-777-1847 www.gospelcom.net

Gospel Films Publications, the publishing arm of
Gospel Films, Inc. P.O. Box 455; Muskegon, MI 49443-0455
616-773-3361 1-800-253-0413 Fax: 616-777-1847

Visit us on the World Wide Web at
http://www.gospelcom.net

ISBN 1-55568-201-4

GFP Catalog #GFP0003
First Printing, June 1997

Printed in the United States of America

*To
Colette,
and our children—*

*Nathaniel,
Collin,
Nicholas,
and
Chloë Marie*

May you always dance in the light…

This book is a compilation of thoughts that have been running around in my head for many years. They arrived there through the educational process, through conversations with colleagues, clients, friends, family, and God. The thoughts and ideas have changed over the years, and as they have, a myriad of changing feelings has occurred simultaneously. Some comforting, some troubling, yet all essential in assisting me through my own journey toward health and wellness, out of the shadows and into an ever brightening light. It has only been through the healthy sustaining relationships that I have developed over those years that this book was possible.

This book is first and foremost the product of prayer and God's guidance. To Him I give the glory. I would also like to thank my parents, Leon and Delores Beighley, for their love, support, and the positive consistency of their walk with God. It set an example that, although I journeyed away from it, called me back in non-judgmental and loving ways. I would like to acknowledge my sisters, Janet Moreen, Susan Whittum, and Linda Luckey, not only for their prayers and support, but also for providing me the insights regarding how our family functioned as we all grew up together. Our family certainly wasn't "perfect", but it was "perfect for me." I would like to acknowledge Dr. John Mulder for his assistance in formulating the outline for this project and his input on Chapter 1. I could have not completed this book without the encouragement of dear friends Margaret Enos, and Chuck and Peggy Mulder. They encouraged continually, pushed when pushing was necessary, and laughed at all the appropriate places.

A special acknowledgment and thanks to Rev. Billy Zeoli, President of Gospel Films, Inc. for his belief in a project that some would consider to be "too secular to be spiritual" and others would consider to be "too spiritual to be secular." His guidance and friendship, and the support of his wonderful staff, allowed this project to become the reality I always believed it could be.

I would also like to thank Dr. Kenneth H. Louden, my mentor, my partner, my friend, my guidance counselor, and my father-figure in the absence of my own. He believed in me even when I didn't believe in myself. He recognized what God had in store for me and refused to give up—even when that would have been the easiest thing to do.

Finally, the support of Colette, Nicholas, and Chloë was the foundation for this book. Nicholas and Chloë were the cheerleaders who asked daily, "What chapter are you on now, Daddy?" Colette's clinical expertise and insights as a fellow family therapist and loving wife were essential and invaluable in helping me "look through another window" to see concepts and conundrums that filled in the missing pieces I was struggling to find. Her editing skills made me look good regardless of where I inaccurately placed my punctuation. Like Ken Louden, she supported and loved me through 12 years of struggle and turmoil, always believing in the wonderment that "I" and "WE" could experience as we moved out of the shadows. She showed me that passion was not reserved only for love, but for all of Life as well. That's a debt I could never repay.

Thank you for your patience, your love, your support—and putting up with the tirades of a husband and father as he occasionally experienced "writer's block" and hid behind the computer screen for what seemed like forever. Colette, I apologize for the nightly "tossing and turning." Maybe we can both get some sleep now. I love you...

The book is done—let's all dance!

TABLE OF CONTENTS

Foreword

W hen you meet someone for the first time, there are a few natural questions that you ask of each other:

What's your name?
What do you do?
Where are you from?

In this powerful and helpful book, my friend David Beighley helps all of us understand the extraordinary importance of knowing—really knowing—"where you are from."

He takes us on a tour through our personal geography; a trip not to a physical place on a map but rather into the lessons of our past. With gentle insistence, he shows us how the past really is a prologue for our behavior. Then he points the way to a future not clouded by backward glances and dark shadows, but filled rather with optimism, growth and the Light that penetrates the deepest darkness - the grace and forgiveness of a loving God.

Our yesterdays can and do influence what today and tomorrow will be like for us.

We are shaped by parents . . . who were shaped by their parents . . . who in turn were shaped by their parents . . . and so it has been from the sorrowful moment that Adam yielded to sin in the Garden of Eden.

Adam, after all, represents both the crowning achievement of God's creation and the embodiment of what it means to be broken, dependent and human. He is, for better and for worse, the patriarch - the head - of the "family of origin" for each one of us.

Through the generations events occur and experiences are encountered that profoundly impact us—for better and for worse. We cannot deny our past, but we must not be bound by our past. We need to learn from its lessons, and, in the process, break the patterns of destructive emotions and behaviors that we inherited.

This book delves deeply into the human condition. It goes beyond the self-help, how-to formula. It is a gift of common sense and uncommon love from a Christian counselor. David Beighley shows the way to "get past our past" and move forward in healthy and healing ways not merely in our individual lives, but also in our relationships with God and others.

As a man whose world view is unmistakably Christian, he relies on twin sources of strength:

The ancient wisdom of the Scriptures
and
the modern insights of psychology.

David Beighley is, by training and profession, a pastor, a family therapist and a counselor. His keen mind is balanced by a tender and loving heart. He is a friend who demonstrates his concern and care for those who are willing to confront the shadows of their past and build positive and productive lives for the future.

I am thrilled that now, through this book and companion video series, David's insights may be magnified many times over, resulting in healthy and happy lives for many more people.

I am grateful to God that David's abilities, combined with the dedication of the attentive reader of this book, will allow us to discover not only where we are "from," but also where we, in faith, are going.

It is my prayer that as you read this book you will gain not only strength but also joy for the exciting adventure of your life in the future.

In His love and mine,

Billy Zeoli
President of Gospel Films, Inc.

Prologue

"For I have chosen him,
so that he will direct his children
and his household after him
to keep the way of the Lord
by doing what is right and just,
so that the Lord will bring about for Abraham
what he has promised him."
–Genesis 18:19 NIV

"If you cannot get rid of
the family skeleton,
you may as well
make it dance"
–George Bernard Shaw

There is a tale of a scorpion and a swan who met one day. Some say it was a scorpion and a turtle, or a scorpion and a duck, but the important player in this tale is the scorpion. For the sake of this story, we'll say it was a swan he met.

It seems that in his travels the scorpion came upon a large body of water. Because scorpions don't swim, he contemplated just how he would get across. While he was thinking about his dilemma, a swan happened by and the scorpion saw his chance for transportation across the water.

"Stately swan," he called, "please come to me and give me passage across the water, for you glide so easily and I cannot swim."

"No, that is not possible," replied the swan. "For if I get too close to you, you will sting me and I will surely die."

"That's not so," scoffed the scorpion. "If I were to sting you while we were crossing the water, then I myself would drown. Please come grant me passage."

The swan considered this logic and slowly made her way to the shore where the scorpion climbed upon her back, and they began to cross the water.

All of a sudden, in the middle of this body of water, the scorpion swung his large tail around and stung the swan. And as the swan was dying and the scorpion drowning, the swan looked over sadly and asked, "But, why?" The drowning scorpion shrugged before disappearing beneath the water's surface and replied, "I don't know. I guess it's just my nature."

Each day individuals enter therapy offices worldwide and share the "almost successes" which are subsequently followed by turmoil and tragedy. The man who is in line for a major promotion at work decides to go on an alcoholic binge and destroys his chances for advancement. The wife, whose husband lavishes her with a cruise for their tenth anniversary, has an affair shortly after their return, destroying trust within the relationship. Or the honor roll student heading for the all-state golf team only to have his grades disintegrate, and he becomes academically ineligible.

Each individual stands at the door of success.

They have worked diligently to get there. They often have the full support and open admiration of well-wishing family and friends. And yet, as they approach the potential fulfillment of their quest, their arrival is accompanied by an inner tension and anxiety that far exceeds the normal excitement of achievement. It is an overwhelming need to run, to escape, to hide from the success they are in imminent danger of achieving. And when asked the unavoidable question, "But, why?" they respond with a voice of universal resignation and distress, "I don't know. *I guess it's just my nature.*" And they proceed to drown in the tragedy of an unconscious compulsion to *not succeed.*

This book is the pathway out of the shadows of confusion and into the light of certainty for everyone who balks at the approach of success in their lives. It clearly reveals the life-premise at work in every person's life—that, almost invariably, *behavior is functional.* What this translates into is "nobody does nothin' for nothin'," and that our behavior has a specific function and purpose in our lives. This behavior is firmly grounded in our personhood and comes about as a result of both the overt and covert, verbal and nonverbal messages we received in our families of origin. It is in this place that, out of an intense sense of *family loyalty,* we each "fit" in an effort to sustain the family order. This is not always done in positive, healthy ways. It is often done in destructive ways designed to aid the family in maintaining its own personal level of dysfunction. And while the behavior may have served its specific purpose in history, we very often unconsciously carry the behaviors into adult life, living out history in the present, and passing the behaviors onto another unsuspecting generation—our children. And, if not challenged or changed, we will see in them the mirror image of our own frustrations, pain, and dysfunction. This book will help *you* understand and consciously counter the "shadows" of your past in which you unconsciously perform an ongoing dance, perpetuating the challenges and struggles you face on a daily basis.

Dancing with Yesterday's Shadows is a three-phased attack on our unproductive and prohibiting behaviors: Education, Identification, and Re-creation.

In the Education phase you will learn about the *Dance*—the dynamics of family systems and about functional (and often dysfunctional) behaviors which rise out of a deep sense of family loyalty. We will discuss the multigenerational impact of family loyalty to unconscious messages and predestined behaviors. We hope you will then achieve a deeper understanding and sense of how these behaviors have sustained themselves through the generations, and where they are rooted. It is through this education process that the journey toward and through the door of success begins.

The Identification phase of this work focuses on the *Shadows*—the specific past and present behaviors that are creating significant roadblocks to your successes, one situation at a time and one day at a time. We will create a window into the past generation to aid in determining what behaviors didn't work then and what meanings those behaviors and messages held at that time in your life. We will then bring attention to what each individual has brought with them into their new relationships, marriages, and families subsequent to leaving their family of origin. We will investigate the impact of family-of-origin issues on our selections of mates, friends, and professions, and even on a relationship with God. We also will discuss what occurs when a relationship (i.e., marriage, friendship, partnership) occurs between individuals who have unconscious or conscious unresolved issues in their family of origin. Lastly, in this section, we will discuss how the current family system reflects family-of-origin dysfunction and how that dysfunction is passed on to our own children.

Finally, the Re-creation phase of this work, the *Light,* is specifically designed to help you in consciously and behaviorally breaking the cycle of dysfunctional loyalty. This section of the journey begins with techniques of becoming more acutely aware of the loyalty patterns. It then addresses methods of making specific decisions to become appropriately disloyal to the dysfunctional traits. Next, the very important issue of *needs* will be evaluated. We must each become aware that relationships are based on needs. After all, if we didn't have needs we wouldn't be in relationships because they are *just too much work!* Methods for evaluating and pursuing needs in a healthy and constructive way will be presented and discussed. This section will also direct attention to the process of creating new and healthy loyalties in our lives and relationships. Finally, you will learn how to overtly teach your children about creating healthy loyalties in order that they may freely and boldly approach the doors of their dreams and walk through unencumbered by the dysfunction of the past.

The journey toward healthy living is not an easy one. There are many hurts, struggles, and unresolved issues that provide obstacles. However, the journey itself is far less difficult than the ongoing turmoil of the "It's just my nature to not succeed" which plagues so many people every day of their lives. As we take the journey together, we must remember that the successes can be ours—if we are willing to walk through the door.

This book addresses clinical issues which plague each one of us from time to time. It addresses spiritual issues which we struggle with in our search for personal meaning in our lives, power that is greater than we are to give us hope, and a respite from the enigmatic tendency to do what is unhealthy even though we know, most of the time, what is healthy for our lives. It includes many stories of individuals and families who are on this journey toward wellness. The stories I share often become mirrors to illumine the pathways toward growth and fulfillment for the reader. These anecdotes do not necessarily represent specific individuals I see in my clinical practice, but are sometimes composites of cases I have witnessed during 20 years of treating individuals, couples, and families. All names, and often the gender and ages of subjects referred to in this book, have been changed to protect the rights to privacy of each individual.

Included throughout this book are a series of **Shadowchasers,** exercises designed to help you examine your past, stretch your imagination, challenge your perceptions and beliefs, and create a healthy and whole vision for your future. These are not tasks to be "done" so that you can advance in the book, but rather events to be savored, rays of light to be basked in and enjoyed as they reveal the hidden elements of Who You Are, and give you a glimpse of Who You Can Be.

This book is written from an unabashedly and unapologetically God-centered perspective. In writing a book of this nature there is always an opportunity to create a good "clinical" work that in some way dilutes the spiritual perspective in the process. Or, there is the opposite opportunity to deliver a good "spiritual" work in which the necessary clinical elements are overshadowed and under-played. In this book you will note the spiritual references throughout the chapters delivered in conjunction with the clinical anecdotes. It is my firm belief that healthy growth is *not possible* in the absence of a strong spiritual base and consistent "God-connection." Within ourselves we are not capable of sustaining healthy personhood or solid relationships if we have somehow become a power unto ourselves. Our connection with the Almighty Higher Power is the only source of dependable strength.

My hope and prayer is that this book will help each reader create a map to guide them in following their own healthy physical, mental, and spiritual journey. The journey begins with a decision to walk through the door into the unknown of all you could be... if you chose.

The door is in front of you.

It's time to walk through.

CHAPTER 1

The Sum of the Parts...

"I have no greater joy
than to hear that my children
are walking in the truth."
–III John 1:4   NIV

"Who of us is mature enough for offspring
before the offspring themselves arrive?
The value of marriage is not that
adults produce children
but that children produce adults."
–Peter De Vries

Nathaniel was three years old when he captured his first worm. This wasn't one of the small red worms one often finds when working in the yard. It was a very large nightcrawler about five inches long, and he was ecstatic about his conquest. He brought it into the house and proudly displayed the trophy to his mother, who suggested that worms were an "outdoor project" and quickly ushered him back outside. Sometime later, checking on him to see how he had fared with his worm, we found that he had taken a small stick and skillfully cut the worm into four sections. Unmistakably there were two larger pieces and two smaller pieces. He looked up with a gleeful grin on his face and cheerfully announced, "*Look!* I made a *family.*"

Family. It's a common word, used daily by almost every one of us. A simple word, but complex enough to conjure up many different images in each person's mind.

Family
Kith and kin
Flesh and blood
Tribe and nation.
Religion and Sect.

The term carries with it a special meaning for everyone who is part of the human race.

For the past several decades the definition and configuration of the family has undergone very dramatic shifts and changes. It has taken on a progressively complex character. For example, during World War II, housewives and mothers went into the factories and plants to support the war effort. My wife's grandmother was a housewife until, when her husband was called to war, she went to work in a shipyard, the kind of work that had been previously reserved for men—the traditional "breadwinners" of the family. The war initiated a trend that placed more and more women permanently into the workplace. As a result, the care of children was placed in the hands of baby-sitters, childcare providers, and school systems. A new term was developed to describe those children who returned home from school each day to an empty house until their dual-career parents returned from work— "latch-key children."

Another dramatic shift was the return to caring for elderly parents in our homes. Geriatric parents unable to sufficiently care for themselves often were forced to rely on full financial and physical support from their adult children. This often placed additional financial strains on the family necessitating additional jobs to increase the income to a "sustaining level." Family members found themselves caring for Grandma and Grandpa, although not always voluntarily or willingly. When an elderly parent comes into an adult child's home to live, the entire way in which the family functions changes dramatically. There are issues of privacy, space, leadership of the home, personality conflicts, unhealthy alliances, financial concerns, and often vast communication disparities which lead to fear, hurt feelings, and mistrust in the relationships. More than a few divorces have come about as a result of not being able to handle a parent moving into the nuclear family.

Shadowchaser

THINK ABOUT YOUR OWN FAMILY ORIGIN. CAN YOU
REFLECT BACK ON THREE EVENTS THAT YOU BELIEVE HAD
A SIGNIFICANT IMPACT IN SHAPING THE WAY THE FAMILY
WORKED TOGETHER AS A UNIT (I.E., DEATH OF A PARENT,
RECEIVING A MONETARY WINDFALL, DRUG OR ALCOHOL
ABUSE, OR CHURCH INVOLVEMENT, ETC.)?

In yet another shift, medical science began creating life in test tubes,
artificially inseminating women who would otherwise be childless. Tech-
nological advances have even allowed for surrogate mothering, providing
a "rental womb" for women unable to maintain a pregnancy. A joke which
circulated during the beginning stages of that technology went as follows:

Question: *"What's the advantage of being a 'test tube' baby?"*
Answer: *"You get a 'womb with a view.'"*

The legal system also has played a significant role in redefining the family. Issues of adoption, divorce, blended families (made up of "his, hers, and
ours"), live-in relationships, out-of-wedlock pregnancies and births, homosexual unions—all of these factors have significantly increased within American society, indelibly changing the definitions of the family as we know
it. In two high-profile cases, judges in Michigan and Florida totally rede-
fined the meaning of *family* for Baby Jessica and Kimberly Mayes. In one
California case the courts were forced to decide custody in a situation where
one woman was artificially inseminated by another woman with the aid of
a turkey baster and the sperm of the second woman's brother. Who were
the parents? Who should have custody? Who were the grandparents? When
the relationship between the two women disintegrated, the fate of a confused child went to the courts. These shifts in defining the concept of
family are not only changing the nature of relationships, but they are also
changing the way in which family and social systems function. There are
issues before the courts today, such as insurance benefits for homosexual
partners and the recognition of homosexual marriages by individual states.
Clearly, the definition of "family" is in a state of flux never before seen in
our culture.

In order to make the discussion of family systems a bit easier, let's break that concept down into four distinct groups: nuclear family, family of origin, extended family, and the family as a "system."

We will define the *nuclear family* as the parents and their children ordinarily living in one household throughout the child's early development and school-age period. This definition also would include those maintaining two households in the case of separated or divorced parents. We also will include in the nuclear family household step-parents and step-children through remarriage or any other relatives or persons whose physical or emotional attachments to the family members are equivalent to those typically found between biologically related parents and children.

We will describe *family of origin* as the nuclear family in which the adult individual was raised. In other words, it is the family you "grew up in." Family of origin is most often the label given to the family in which you spent your formative years, birth through seven or eight years. If a death or divorce took place during that time, and remarriages occurred, it is possible that more than one father-figure or mother-figure existed within the context of your family of origin. The family of origin also can include step-siblings and half-siblings if those additions to the family took place during the formative years.

Extended family is defined as any and all biological relatives and relations through marriage including uncles, aunts, cousins, family of origin, and nuclear family. In our definition of extended family we also will include all the friends and persons in the community with whom the family members have ongoing face-to-face relationships of some emotional or physical significance. This would include what we commonly refer to as the "church family" or the "family of God," those individuals with whom we hold a common spiritual bond.

Lastly, *family system* refers to the process by which these individuals function as a "whole," what drives or motivates them, what establishes their value system as a group, and their interactive dynamics, i.e., the impact of each person's attributes, attitudes, and behaviors on the rest of the family.

As we look at these definitions, we can plainly see that families can be *created*—connected not by blood, but by circumstance and choice. Additionally, this entity which we call *family* has a life of its own, independent of the individuals involved. To be sure, in the case of the family system, the total is much more than the sum of the parts.

In this book, when I refer to *family*, it includes the following characteristics:

1. A collection of people living under the same roof who impact each

other on a regular basis. For example, this could include Mr. and Mrs. Anderson, their 15-year-old son, their 17-year-old daughter, and Mr. Anderson's 87-year-old mother who recently was widowed and has come to live with them.

2. Those related by blood or marriage who may not live in the same household, but still have influence in a person's life. This would include Mr. Anderson's sister, who lives in the same town as they do, and Mrs. Anderson's two brothers and their wives, who live across the country, but speak weekly on the phone, and visit at least once a year.

3. Individuals *un*related by blood but integrally entwined by situation. Some of the consulting I do is with The Better Life Institute in Grand Rapids, Michigan. This is a consulting firm which is owned and operated by a *very* Italian family. Not long after I began working there, not only was I invited to functions, but my wife and children were included also. They remembered my children's birthdays, invited them to teas, included us in family outings and events—all of the things one might expect to experience as part of a family. And although there was no relationship by blood, my children consistently refer to "Gramma Pat," "Uncle Ted," and "Aunt Mary." As a result of the depth and relevance of the relationships to all of us, there is no doubt but that they qualify as "family." We also have family of this type on the West coast, where we lived for ten years, far away from my nuclear family. There is Aunt Margaret, Uncle Harvey and Aunt Michelle, and others who adopted us into their families as "honorary members." Our lives entwined deeply as a result of interactions we have had, and the significance of those relationships could not be any deeper if they *had* been biological.

Recently, the term *dysfunctional* has been used to describe the unhealthy behaviors and traits that exist in a family system. Since there are no "perfect" earthly families, every family carries within itself the *capability* and *tendency* for dysfunction. In fact, because of our imperfections, no absolute definition of either normal or dysfunctional is possible. While God's Word provides definitive guidelines for us, they are just that—guidelines for being as healthy as our humanness allows. Therefore, we must cautiously refer to dysfunctional behaviors as *those actions and behaviors which create an unusual degree of stress or distress to an individual or individuals within a particular family system.* As the distress intensifies, it creates an imbalance or rift in the *usual* or *expected* level of functioning in the family. This "usual and expected" level of functioning is referred to as *homeostasis*. Homeostasis may occur at any point on the continuum of health or pathology within that family. This may be difficult to conceptualize, but consider a line with dysfunction on one end and health on the other. It might look something like this:

DYSFUNCTION_____HEALTH

What we don't really know is where dysfunction leaves off or where health begins. All we know is that the farther to the left we go, the more dysfunctional the family system, and that the farther to the right we go, the more healthy the family system. Because every family is different, the degrees of health or dysfunction also will be different. Additionally, we have to factor in *homeostasis,* or that "usual and expected" level of functioning we referred to earlier.

For example, in a family of bank robbers, a member who decided to become a minister and lead a life of integrity would greatly distress the other family members and threaten the homeostasis of this "criminal" family system. In order to regain the homeostasis, the bank robbing family members would have to either talk their ministry-bound sibling back into the family trade *or* eject him from the family. It is in this fashion that the family maintains its *usual* level of functioning.

Because the concept of homeostasis is so important in understanding the behaviors in family systems, I am going to share three anecdotes to further illustrate the homeostatic process.

The Case of the Diminished Chord

My middle sister, Sue, is a very accomplished pianist. As a teen she purchased a baby grand piano which occupied a space in the living room of our home just under her second floor bedroom. The piano was a cherished piece of furniture and she kept it dusted, waxed, and had a velvet key cover to keep the dust from the ivories. She has always had an excellent mind for music theory, and an excellent ear for "what comes next" in terms of musical progression. On one occasion, upon returning very late from a date, I walked over to the piano, carefully and quietly lifted the lid, removed the key cover, and played—just loudly enough for her to hear—a diminished chord. Now, a diminished chord is one of those musical anomalies that just doesn't sound good by itself. It needs a subsequent chord to make it "complete." After having completed the deed, I replaced the key cover, closed the lid, and walked quietly up to my bedroom which was next to hers.

And I waited.

It wasn't even two minutes later when I heard her bedroom door open, and heard her pad down the hallway in her slippers, down the stairs to the piano, lift the lid, remove the key cover—and finish the chord progression.

The next morning she was furious. "How could you do that to me?" she demanded. "You knew I couldn't stand it if you didn't finish the progression. I just laid there in bed waiting, and waiting, and waiting—until I couldn't stand it anymore. Don't you *ever* do that to me again." This is a rather comical example of the anxiety that occurs when the "normal" or "expected" behaviors do not occur, and the homeostasis is not maintained.

The Case of the Restocked Liquor Cabinet

A couple came to see me on the brink of divorce. They had been married for twenty-five years and during every year of the marriage the husband had been a practicing alcoholic. As a result of his disease and unwillingness to be in recovery, the wife had single-handedly raised the children, paid the bills, arranged to have things done around the house she could not do and could not depend on him to do, attended the parent-teacher conferences, cleaned up his messes after his binges, put him to bed, and made excuses for him at work. She stated she had stayed in the marriage for the sake of her four children. Now, however, the last of the children had left home and she was done with the marriage. She had announced to him that she was giving him one chance to engage in active recovery and to stop drinking completely, or she was leaving him. This sufficiently frightened the husband who vowed to get into counseling and recovery to stay married, and he acknowledged that she had taken care of him all of his adult life, and that he needed to learn to take care of himself. We admitted the husband into an alcohol recovery center and he did very well. He attended regular AA meetings, began developing healthy relationships with his adult children and their children, making amends for the impact of his disease on their lives, and began taking initiative and responsibility around the home and in the family finances. By all standards he was doing extremely well. However, a strange phenomenon began to occur.

The healthier and happier he became, the more depressed his wife became.

Six months after his recovery began, he came home from work one evening to find his wife waiting at the door, more cheerful than she had been lately. She told him, "You've been doing so well with your drinking that I think you've got it licked, and I've got a surprise for you." She took him into the dining room and showed him that she had *completely restocked his liquor cabinet!* Within two months they were back where they started, and were "miserably happy."

She had developed their entire relationship, and based her own sense of self, on her ability to take care of him, and even though she outwardly hated it, his alcoholism was a way for her to have purpose, self-esteem, and control over the family. His health was a direct threat to her need to control and the homeostasis of the family system.

The Case of the Hard-to-Place Child

Leroy was an angry 10-year-old. He had come from a highly destructive and abusive family and he, along with his younger brother and sister, had been taken from that family. It was my job to assist in finding a foster care placement for Leroy. I found a home where I felt he would receive the care and guidance he so badly needed in his life. And he went. He lasted about three months before the family called and said that he was so disruptive and destructive in their family that they would have to send him back. I found him another home. Three months later it was the same story. He was out of control, they had given it their best shot, and he had to be returned. Over the period of three years, Leroy was placed in six homes, all with the same result. Frustrated, I called this now 13-year-old into my office and said, "Leroy, I don't get it. I'm doing everything I can to find you good places to be and you keep blowing it! What's the deal?" The young teen looked up at me, and told me something I sorely needed to hear. "Look, Doc," he said, "I know how to handle it when my dad comes home drunk. I know how to handle it when my mom is chasing me around the house with a stick or a knife. I know how to handle it when my mom and dad don't come home for a couple of days and I have to take care of my brother and my sister. But I *don't* know how to handle it when somebody wants to hug on me, or kiss on me, or do stuff for me." Leroy taught me a very valuable lesson:

> *There is comfort in pain when pain is all you've known.*

Leroy expected to be abused and neglected. He knew that this was his life—what he could expect. And when it didn't happen, his anxiety went up to the point where *he* would create the chaos—what he was used to— and it was actually a relief. He created his own turmoil to maintain a sense of personal homeostasis.

Shadowchaser

THINK OF THE WAYS YOUR FAMILY SYSTEM MAINTAINS HOMEOSTASIS. WHAT IS THE HEALTHIEST TRAIT THAT YOUR FAMILY CONSISTENTLY EXHIBITS (I.E., REGULAR FAMILY DEVOTIONS, TIME AS A UNIT, SPORTS, PRAYER, ETC.)?

THINK THROUGH WHAT YOU BELIEVE IS THE MOST DYSFUNCTIONAL TRAIT THAT YOUR FAMILY EXHIBITS (I.E., INTERMITTENT OR REGULAR SUBSTANCE ABUSE, VERBAL, PHYSICAL, OR EMOTIONAL ABUSE, ETC.)?

IF YOU COULD HAVE CHANGED ONLY ONE THING ABOUT HOW YOUR FAMILY OPERATED WHILE YOU WERE GROWING UP, WHAT WOULD THAT HAVE BEEN?

Obviously, there are a variety of ways in which families and family systems function in an attempt to maintain order and homeostasis. There are several concepts which describe these different characteristics. The specific purpose of each concept is to keep the family operating at its own, unique level of functioning. Regardless of how the processes play themselves out in the system, our awareness of the concepts will help identify which process(es) may be occurring in our own lives and family systems. This can and will ultimately provide us an opportunity for positive and healthy change.

Concept 1: Each family is an "interdependent system."

A change in one family member's action will influence and be simultaneously influenced by the actions of all other family members. A word picture that I often use to describe this concept is that of a watch. Not a digital, but the old type with its many gears of all different sizes. If just *one* tooth on *one* gear, regardless of its size or function in the watch, was to break off, the entire watch would keep time differently. It would change how every other gear functioned, even those gears it was not directly in contact with. It also works this way in the family. Issues like sickness, terminal illness, unemployment, a change in job status or income, a child leaving home to go to school, marriage, divorce and remarriage—all of these will have a direct impact on the way the family system operates, physically, emotionally, and very often spiritually. It is not necessarily only the negative stimuli which can impact the family. *Any* change will have an impact. There have been many articles in the newspapers and magazines about individuals who have won the lottery, or become rich by some other means, and how, despite every effort to maintain the lifestyle to which they were accustomed, their lives and families were literally turned upside down by the event. *All* the parts have a direct impact on all the other parts of a family system.

Concept 2: Each family writes its own rules.

Every family is "rule-governed" and the family members create a set of rules (which can be spoken or unspoken) that tend to maintain their interactions within a relatively fixed range. There are rules regarding every issue that arises within the family and even if they are unspoken, they are still "acted" upon. For example, in my family of origin the church was an integral part of the family life. I have three younger sisters, and we all agree we received the same "message," or rule, regarding church. That particular rule came from my father, with the full unspoken support of my mother. The rule was as follows: "You will be in church *every time the doors are open.* Church supersedes athletic events, social events, band concerts, or anything else that comes up. If there is a conflict, *you* will be in church." It was in the establishment, enforcement, understanding, and adherence to this rule that helped the family maintain its "spiritual homeostasis."

Concept 3: Each family creates its own language and way of communicating.

All verbal and nonverbal behavior in any situation is communication. There is a "law" of communication in family therapy that dictates, *"One cannot **not** communicate."* If there is inconsistent or incongruent communication over time, the result can be heightened anxiety and confusion in the family system which often leads to "disturbed behavior." Clarifying communication is extremely important both in healthy families and while interacting with other systems outside of the family.

I recall an instance when a client came in on a Monday morning and indicated that she had seen my family and me at a large, local store over the weekend. "I was going to come up and say, 'Hi'," she stated, "but you had this look on your face that said, 'Don't even *think* about talking to me'." Embarrassed, I assured her that my demeanor was not personal, that I had not seen her, and that she could feel free at any time to talk with me wherever she might encounter me.

That evening, after I got home, I shared the story with my wife, Colette. "A woman came in today and said she saw us at the store over the weekend, and that she was going to come over and speak with me, but that I had a look about me that made me very unapproachable. What do you think about that?" I asked. After brief consideration she slowly said, "Yessss. That's your *'shopping face.'* You know how much you hate to shop. When we're there, you typically have a look about you that lets people know you are not a happy camper." I was totally unaware of the messages I was sending the people around me with my "behavioral" language. I was aware, however, that I didn't want to continue to send that kind of a message, especially since it could be so easily misinterpreted. So, I told my wife, "I was unaware I was doing that. And I don't *want* to do that. But, apparently it is not in my conscious awareness that this occurs, so I'm going to need your help. If you see me doing that would you please let me know." She assured me she would, and as recently as a few weeks ago, while we were shopping, she turned to put something in the cart, looked up and smiled, and said, "You're doing it…" And sure enough, I was. Out of the awareness of the dysfunctional language, I was able to continue my journey of making my behavioral language and my verbal language congruent.

Concept 4: Each family has its own style of conflict management.

In the family, each member develops individual styles of managing differences. Each individual brings into a conflict their own perception of the conflict. The differences in these perceptions of what the conflict "looks like" must be recognized before the conflict can be resolved. Some families manage conflict by yelling or screaming, or by physical intimidation or abuse. Others manage conflict by withdrawal, isolation, or the "passive-aggressive" format of "sooner or later, I'll make you pay for that." Other, healthier families talk things out, looking for mutually acceptable resolutions, not putting the issue to rest until all parties have something they can live with.

In addition to the format of conflict resolution is the need to make sure we are addressing the core issue of the conflict. When a couple is arguing about a particular purchase, the wife may believe that she is arguing about shape, size, color, etc., and the husband may not care about any of those things, but is arguing his position in an effort not to be "controlled" by a wife whom he believes is trying to dictate to him what he can or cannot do in a particular situation. Unless those individuals can come to terms with *the meaning of the behavior* at the core, or just underneath the surface, of their argument, no real or lasting resolution is possible.

One young couple coming into therapy said that one of their biggest recent battles was over the matter of coming into treatment with me. She wanted to—and he didn't! She believed his reticence was based on fear of being vulnerable, fear of losing control, and the fact that he would be threatened by being in therapy with another man. His entire focus for *not* wanting to go into therapy was that he believed the cost was prohibitive. And, yet, they had been unable to get at those points. They were stuck at—"We need to go" and "No we don't."

Concept 5: Each *healthy* couple learns ways to resolve marital conflict and act as a united parental team.

The well-functioning family has a strong parental alliance. Coupleship is based on acceptance of individual differences between the spouses, successful conflict management, and the meeting of another's needs as much as is possible. In the healthy family this is the strongest alliance in the system. The children become aware that mom and dad speak with "one voice," and that they are going to be engaged in ongoing dialogue regarding decisions around the house, and that getting an answer from one of them will be the same as getting the answer from the other. This diminishes the opportunity for manipulation and playing one parent against the other in the family. I remember as a young boy going up to my father in church on Sunday with a friend at my side and asking if that friend could come home and have dinner with us. If the answer was "no," this would put my father in an embarrassing situation, so I figured with my friend present, the only alternative my father had was to say "yes." That first time he did. But after my friend had gone home, he and my mother sat me down and told me how the game would be played from that point on. "If you come to us alone, and give us the opportunity to discuss it together, you will always have the possibility of our saying yes to your request. But, if you ever bring a friend with you to ask the question, and put either of us on the spot like that again, the answer will automatically be no, even if we would have said yes had you come to us alone." With that alliance they removed an opportunity for me to manipulate them or play one against the other. I have found that "one voice" concept very valuable with my own children as they, like all normal developing children, have tried their hand at "divide and conquer."

I have also learned that there are very few communication "emergencies" with children. Despite their projected sense of urgency ("But, I have to know *right now!*"), there is typically enough time to say, "Your mother and I will talk it over and give you an answer as soon as we can." In a healthy marriage the couple will actively pursue opportunities to show themselves as a united front.

When this alliance does not occur, persistent styles of submerged, unresolved, or competitive marital conflict may give rise to distance and loneliness in the marriage. It also presents the possibility of physical or psychological dysfunction, triangled involvement of the children as an inappropriate and often unwilling partner to either parent, or an outside party in an inappropriate alliance or liaison, such as in the case of an affair. When spouses are unable to resolve and contain their conflicts within the marital relationship, a child may be "triangled" in, or join in, to resolve the conflict. The child's involvement serves to deflect attention away from the conflict, or swing the balance of power from one parent to the other.

Several years ago I received a call from a man asking if I would see his teenage daughter in therapy. I asked him what the issues were and he shared with me that the girl was "out of control," not coming home at night by curfew, sometimes not coming home at all, dating "older boys" they didn't approve of, skipping school, dressing like a "tramp," and acting disrespectfully and disobediently toward her parents. He assured me that these were not ordinary adolescent acting-out behaviors, but behaviors that went so far against what he and his wife believed in that if a solution were not found to "control" his daughter, they were going to have to remove her from the house. We scheduled an appointment and at the given time this man, his wife, and their only child walked into my office. The father was dressed in a dark business suit, white shirt and tie, and looked very professional. His demeanor, however, was angry, tough, and demanding. The mother was dressed in a shapeless, dark brown dress, shoulder length straight brown hair and no makeup, and her gaze never lifted very far off the ground. She looked quiet, "plain," afraid, and depressed. They were followed by their daughter who looked as though she had just stepped off the cover of a fashion magazine. Her clothes were colorful, fit to reveal every shape she had, her hair was very stylish, and her jewelry accented perfectly the rest of her outfit. She looked confident, strong, and defiant. It was at this point, reading the intake form, that I discovered that this "woman-child" in my office was only 14 years old.

The father did most of the talking, reiterating in front of his wife and daughter what he had shared with me over the phone. When I asked the mother if she shared the perceptions of her husband regarding their daughter, she simply nodded affirmatively. When I addressed the same question to the daughter, she only shrugged. A short time later I asked the parents to leave the office so I could speak with their daughter alone. After they had left, I turned to her and said, "You know, when you walked into the office I had you pegged at 18 or 19 years old. I couldn't believe you were 14. You must spend every spare penny you have on clothes, makeup, and jewelry." She beamed. "Oh, no," she said, "My mother buys all of it for me. She even taught me how to put the makeup on just right." I then asked her about her behaviors and what she thought they were about for her. She frowned and said, "I don't know what it's about. I know the things I do are wrong, and I feel bad doing them. It's not even like I try to hide what I'm doing. Whenever I get home, I always tell my mother everything I did." I was beginning to get a picture of a fractured marital alliance, so I asked the girl to step out of the office and invited only the mother back in. "You know," I said, "Your daughter shared some curious things with me, and I really need to check them out with you. She told me that you buy her the clothes, makeup, and jewelry, and that you taught her how to dress and look the way she does, and that she shares all of her escapades with you when she returns. Is that factual?" As soon as I shared that information the mother began to sob. It was true—all of it. Then the mother described her marriage. She described her husband as extremely jealous and controlling. She couldn't work outside the home because he was afraid she would find someone else and leave him. When she tried to dress up, wear makeup or jewelry, or fashion her hair, he ridiculed her and called her a "tramp" and a "whore" (some of the same terms he had used to describe the daughter). Because of her religious beliefs she did not see divorce as an option even though she was miserable and felt he was abusing her with his behavior. She felt trapped and as though she had no life—that is, no life outside of her daughter. Through her daughter's acting-out behaviors, the mother was able to have some fun and excitement, and get out from under her dominating husband's control. And the daughter, out of love for her mother and the developmental aspects of adolescence (which consist of pushing the boundaries), was more than happy to oblige. She got to have a "great time" and simultaneously "teach" her mother how to stand up to her father. For neither one of them was this a conscious dynamic. It was the internal, unconscious forces which engaged the family system in the dysfunctional behaviors.

The work with the daughter was minimal. When all three of them understood the dynamics of the family system, mom and dad began to engage in marital therapy to improve their communication, conflict resolution, decrease the anger, jealousy, and animosity in the marriage, and learn new and healthier ways of relating. As they did, the daughter was relieved of her inappropriate role and could "let go" of the acting out behaviors. This was a wonderful example to me of the power of the family system, and how one person's motivations (whether it be the daughter's, mother's OR father's) and unhealthy behaviors could impact the entire family system in very dramatic ways.

Concept 6: Each family has a tendency to transfer and project personal attributes and fault toward other family members.

Individuals in a marriage need to understand what they are bringing into that marriage with them. These attributes may have a positive or negative impact on the marriage and the family system. In a "disturbed behavior" relationship, a partner may choose for a spouse someone who resembles, or is the polar "opposite" of his/her parent, or may mentally/emotionally transfer the qualities of a parent unto the spouse. This also can be done to children in the family system.

There have been numerous instances in therapy when a wife has told me, regarding her husband, "He expects me to be his mother." or "He treats me exactly like I'm his mother." Or, the husband who tells me, "She treats me just like she's my mother." These laments come complete with the lack of awareness that the specific mate selections were *made* on the very basis of those similarities. In our mate selection we have a natural tendency to gravitate toward a spouse who will support the kind of relationships we had in our families of origin, even if—perhaps especially if—those relationships were not particularly healthy, because those previous relationships helped shape the homeostasis we were "used to."

The results of these particular matches are not always negative, and, in fact, there are many enhancing qualities that mates can offer one another to create a stronger and more efficient relationship. For example, a married couple who are friends of mine decided to build a business together building custom wood furniture. While he was very creative and imaginative in design, and was a perfectionist in his woodworking skills, he lacked the personality to meet with the public, "sell" himself and his product, take orders, and follow through on the paperwork. His wife, on the other hand, was a highly verbal and charming woman who was very organized in her mental processes and ability to follow through with a task. In recognizing their own strengths and weaknesses, and accepting the strengths and weaknesses of the other, they were able to create a highly successful team based on differences. It is important to note, however, that without the *awareness* of those strengths and weaknesses, and the knowledge that they "chose" one another based on those differences, the relationship could have turned competitive and combative, with each trying to "change" the other. It was the awareness and the acceptance that made the positive difference in the marriage!

Concept 7: Current Involvement with Family of Origin

Each family is impacted by their current involvement with (or distance from) their families of origin. Ongoing dysfunctional behavior can be a function of the spouse's persistent over-involvement or under-involvement (and corresponding levels of emotional reactivity) with their families of origin. For example, a passive woman *who* marries a dominant man *who* perhaps resembles her father, may rely heavily on emotional support from her mother, *who* learned how to deal and cope with the husband over the length of their marriage. This reliance on the mother has the potential of detracting from the growth process in the marriage, and preventing the couple from working through their own issues in a healthy and positive way.

Susan's father was a workaholic businessman who traveled extensively during the week and was home on the weekends. Thursdays and Fridays were a frenzy around their house because "dad was a perfectionist" and the wife and children had learned that everything had better be "ready for dad" when he got home. That meant the house would be immaculate, his favorite foods and beverages in the refrigerator, and no plans on the calendar so that he would be "free" to do as he pleased. No demands were to be placed on him when he was home, and if something went wrong or needed to be fixed, the rest of the family was expected to "handle it." Susan's mother was a quiet woman who had learned over the years how to manipulate her husband into doing what she wanted him to. The direct approach wouldn't work because of the father's strong personality. So the mother developed a passive-aggressive approach. Since she handled the finances, she was able to hide large amounts of money to purchase what she needed, and to take care of things around the house without telling her husband what had happened. She had a closet of her own, and would hide new clothes, wearing them only when he was not around. She would take "mid-week vacations," telling him she was out with her sister. Susan learned these "tricks of the trade" from her mother, and had them ready when she married Larry.

Larry was a tough-minded businessman, but not a workaholic. When he was at work he worked with passion, and he wanted to have a passionate home life as well. He was quick to state his needs, but just as quick to solicit Susan's needs in any situation. However, because his personality *was* so strong, Susan was afraid he would attempt to dominate her as her father had her mother. As a result, Susan spent a lot of time with her mother, sharing her fears and receiving support for "stashing cash," hiding clothes, and taking off during the week. The result was a breach of trust in the relationship that would not have occurred if Larry and Susan had been able to talk out the issues, rather than Susan relying on her mother for input.

On the other hand, a young couple starting out on their own journey can receive a significant amount of healthy support (and education) from their families of origin in the areas of finance, parenting, communication, and a variety of other issues in which the parents have a great deal of experience. If the appropriate emotional and physical boundaries are set up which allow the young couple to develop independence in the relationships with their families of origin, then that involvement can be very positive and supportive.

Fran and Jim had been married four years and had two small children. Both had grown up in homes where church was an important spiritual and social aspect of family life. A job change moved them to a neighboring town about 45 minutes away from the one in which they had grown up, and in which their parents still lived. There was no church of the denomination in which they had been raised, and when it came time to choose a church, they consulted with both sets of parents. Their parents gave them "input" regarding their choices, but no "advice." And the parents were very supportive of their choice, making it a point to attend their children's church when there was a special service.

When it came time to purchase a home, Fran and Jim sat down with their parents and shared their thoughts about price ranges, neighborhoods, and school systems. Their parents listened and again gave input. The parents even arranged to lend their children some money for a larger down payment. The loan was made legally binding, complete with interest and a payment schedule, but with room for extenuating circumstances should they arise. The families saw each other every couple of weeks, and talked on the phone once or twice a week. There were no surprise visits or dropping in on each other without a call. The relationships were healthy because there was respect, boundaries, acceptance of differences, and a desire to be IN the relationship with the other. It is these types of generational interactions which happen in healthy families.

Concept 8: Healthy families express emotions.

Every family system needs to have a process by which the entire range of emotions can be expressed, openly and freely, with the assurance that even if those emotions are not understood, they will be accepted. Children must be taught *how* to express emotions in such a way that demonstrates regard and respect for the other family members and the situation. Disturbed behavior can be a function of family rules that severely restrict the awareness and open expression of basic human needs. Family rules may prohibit or constrict the appropriate expression of affection, sexuality, joy, sadness, fear, hurt, and anger. I have been involved in several cases where the "good kid" who had never expressed negative emotions previously, had exploded with emotional and physical rage to the shock of everyone around. Invariably, the explosion came about as a result of a family rule that mandated no one, or just one other person (usually the father), had *permission* to exhibit anger. And, because our emotions tend to be intense, confining them will result in stress and anxiety, and those emotions have the tendency to come out in unhealthy or inappropriate ways. Most often they manifest themselves as explosions— the result of not being able to any longer confine them. This typically happens in adolescence, a time when hormones are raging and emotions are running rampant. This, coupled with a natural, developmental desire to be independent and rebel against authority, aids in releasing emotions that were before suppressed in order to be loyal, as well as avoid punishment.

Children learn early how to cope with their emotions, and how to release them in ways that are acceptable to the family system. Recently two small children were taken from their parents, and the parents prosecuted, after the children were videotaped beating each other up. The parents' faulty reasoning was that this process would teach the children how to work out their differences. What messages had the parents received from their families of origin which would have allowed for this kind of inappropriate behavior? That violence and "winning" were the methods of choice in resolving conflict. Taking those messages with them into adulthood could only serve to perpetuate a negative and unhealthy family system.

Children will watch their parents to get a sense of how emotions can (or cannot) be expressed. While visiting with friends at a funeral home I watched the children, some of whom were experiencing a family death for the first time, watching their parents for cues on how to act emotionally. The children whose parents were openly showing grief were also able to demonstrate their feelings of loss. The children whose parents were "holding it together" and acting as though this event was business as usual, tended to be silent and withdraw from the people around them. The children who experienced their parents' reaction to death as a celebration of the deceased individual's life, and the passing from this life to eternal life with God, were most comfortable with the concept of death and could be happy with the result at the same time they were sad for the loss. The display of emotion, or lack thereof, is another aspect of how homeostasis within a family system is maintained. The family will fight to maintain its emotional level. This also applies multi-generationally according to the hierarchy of the family system. Even in my own family it is sometimes amusing to see how individuals change in the presence of mom and dad, or Gramma and Grampa.

Shadowchaser

THINK ABOUT THE ISSUE OF RULES IN YOUR FAMILY OF ORIGIN WHAT WERE THE TWO MOST PREDOMINANT RULES AS YOU REMEMBER THEM?

POLL THE OTHER MEMBERS OF YOUR FAMILY OF ORIGIN REGARDING WHAT THEY PERCEIVED TO HAVE BEEN THE TWO MOST PREDOMINANT RULES. COMPARE AND CONTRAST THE DIFFERENCES.

IN EACH LINE, CHOOSE THE WORD THAT BEST DESCRIBES HOW DECISIONS WERE MADE IN YOUR FAMILY OF ORIGIN.

Quiet	Loud	Chaotic	Abusive
Mutual	Pressure	Guilt	Anger
Love	Control	Compassion	With Disregard
Dictatorship	Consensus	Vote	By default

CONSIDER HOW THE FOLLOWING EMOTIONS WERE SPECIFICALLY AND BEHAVIORALLY EXPRESSED IN YOUR FAMILY OF ORIGIN. WHO EXPRESSED THEM AND HOW?

Anger	Love	Pain	Frustration
Joy	Sadness	Reverence	Guilt

You have begun! In this chapter you learned about what makes up a family and how families operate. In the Shadowchasers you examined how these principles and traits manifested themselves in your own family of origin. What did you learn? Throughout the remainder of this book you will receive both clinical and anecdotal information that will help you better understand and conquer the growth-inhibiting or dysfunctional aspects of your personality and family systems. In this way, you will greatly enhance the possibilities of becoming the kind of individual, and having the kind of family, that God has always intended for you.

Chapter Two will help you develop an even clearer picture of the family you come from and how that impacts who you are.

Come! The journey continues

CHAPTER 2

The Acorn Doesn't Fall too Far from the Tree

*"Listen, my son, to your father's instruction
and do not forsake your mother's teaching.
They will be a garland to grace your head
and a chain to adorn your neck."*
–Proverbs 1:8-9 NIV

*"To bring up a child in the way he should go,
travel that way yourself once in a while."*
–Henry Wheeler Shaw

Imagine, for a moment, approaching a large museum of art. As you enter the front doors you notice that not all of the lights are on inside the museum and the interior is somewhere between light and dark, and full of shadows. You open the front door and walk inside. You can see pictures on the walls, but can't really make out the content. You can see sculptures throughout the room, but are unsure of their design. Then, toward the back of the room you see a rather large sculpture, made up of many figures, with a soft light shining down upon it. You approach the sculpture slowly, and as you draw nearer you notice it is the sculpture of a family. It is bronze, dark, and cold. In the middle of the sculpture you see two adults, facing one another and smiling. In front of each is a child, a boy in front of the mother and a girl in front of the father. They are glaring at each other with raised fists. Between them is another girl, arms outstretched, trying desperately to keep her two siblings away from one another. She is crying, and her mouth seems to be frozen on the word, *"stop!"* Standing apart from this group is another girl, her back turned to the others, arms crossed, looking into the distance. The look is passive, non-committal.

"Curious," you think. "That family seems connected and disconnected all at the same time. It's like the parents are happy, but no one else is. I wonder what it means?"

You continue walking through the halls and see in the distance another sculpture. From afar, it looks similar to the one you just saw. You approach it quietly and then notice, with great surprise, that it is a sculpture of *your own family of origin!* You see your father, mother, perhaps a step-father or step-mother, your siblings—all of them are there. And the design of the sculpture, the material it is made from, the positioning and actions of all of the family members, are laid out to depict how *you* remember your family functioning most of the time.

Take a few moments right now to consider that family sculpture you just visualized with your mind's eye. At what point in your life does the sculpture originate? When you were a small child? School age or adolescence? Just before you left home? Who is standing next to whom? Who is close to whom? Who is distant? Is anyone absent? Are the individuals touching in any way, or is there no contact? What position is each member in? What action are they engaged in? What is the look on each person's face?

Now ask yourself what emotional state your family and each member in it is experiencing at the time of the sculpture. Is there happiness? Sadness? Anger or frustration? Loneliness? Who is experiencing what emotion?

Next, look at each member of that family sculpture and ask yourself, "What do I remember going on with that member which would have contributed to their position in this family sculpture?" There are important questions to ask, such as: Was there a "golden child?" Or a gifted child? Or, perhaps, an acting-out and misbehaving child? Were there physical, emotional, or mental challenges that any individual faced? Were there financial problems, employment issues, or long periods without an income? Did the parents have issues with drugs, alcohol, or other issues that had a negative impact on the family? Was there a divorce in the family, or infidelity and affairs? Was there evidence of abuses, whether physical, emotional, or sexual? Were there pregnancies that were not planned for? Were there step-parents involved, and if so, how did they impact the functioning of the family system? Were the parents strong disciplinarians with strong moral values and beliefs that they taught the children? Was there a strong spiritual connection, a well-defined and consistent relationship with God? Or was there a spiritual void—the absence of a "greater and higher power?"

Was there a strong element of spirituality and faith within the family? Which child was most "like" the father, or most "like" the mother? Did the family have a well-developed support system of friends or extended family? Or were they more withdrawn and interdependent one to the other? What do you see?

Look back at the sculpture once again. This time focus carefully on the figure that is you. Look closely at that person. What are they doing? What is that person thinking?   What role does that person play in the family? How does that person *feel* at the point of the sculpture?

And, lastly, examine your *own* feelings right now. How do you feel having examined your family sculpture. Do you feel joy, satisfaction, or happiness? Is there remorse or sadness? Is there any degree of anger or frustration? Or perhaps a combination of feelings occurring simultaneously. How would you describe what it was like to be *you* in this family? Whatever the feelings *you* are experiencing, they are present as a result of the strong attachment you had to your family of origin. It does not matter if the feelings were positive or negative, the attachment was strong because *you* were an integral part of that family of origin, and played an extremely important role in the maintenance of the family's homeostasis.

We call that attachment . . .

Loyalty

Family loyalty—there is no stronger force within a family system.

The American Heritage Dictionary defines the word "loyal" as *"steadfast in allegiance to one's homeland, government, or sovereign. Faithful to a person, ideal, or custom."* It is in no way difficult to extrapolate that definition to include faithfulness to the homeostasis of the family system in which we grew up. In examining loyalty from a family system's point of view, there are five important considerations. They are as follows:

1. **Each individual in the family sees and experiences the family from a different vantage point.**

2. **Perception is reality. What we *believe* to be true regarding the family or any of the individuals in the family, is what we will act out upon whether or not it has any basis in reality for any of the other family members.**

An interesting story which illustrates the first two points is the tale of the "blind men and the elephant." It seems a number of blind men were led to an elephant and each asked to describe the beast. The one near the side of the elephant shared that it was wide and broad, like a wall. The one near the tail related that it was long and flexible, like a rope. The one near the tusks stated that the others must be mad, for an elephant was sharp, hard, and pointed, like a spear. The one near the legs likened it to a tree, and the one near the trunk to a boa constrictor. The question was then asked, "Which one was right?" To each, there was a sense of rightness depending upon their position to the elephant. Family systems are very similar. Each member perceives and experiences the family depending upon their position—their vantage point—in the family system.

3. **Family loyalty can have either a negative or a positive impact on the family member, but is always present and specifically designed to make the parent(s) "okay," and maintain homeostasis.**

In a family which engages in a high degree of fiscal responsibility, which focuses on a good work ethic and substantial discipline, loyalty to the family would constitute perpetuating those traits, and working hard to make sure that everyone else in the family perpetuated those traits.

In a family in which there was fiscal irresponsibility, lack of discipline, and work consisted of "whatever was available at the time that you couldn't avoid," the homeostasis would support those kinds of behaviors among all of the members, and anyone who tried to "get ahead" would be seen as disloyal and disturbing to the family system.

4. **Family loyalty is a "team effort" that may mean more, or less, to individual members of the family. Not all members have the same investment in the loyal behaviors even though they may consciously or unconsciously engage in them.**

For an example of this point we can return to the family sculpture we visualized at the beginning of this chapter. The key to the interpretation? *The parents never fought!* They didn't have to. They each had recruited one child, the mother a son, and the father a daughter, to do it for them. And the child in the middle was the designated "peace maker" whose job it was to straighten out the fights of her two siblings without parental intervention in order to keep the parents "happy." The other sibling, who wanted no part of the infighting, was expelled from the family and remained on the outside of the system, uninvolved in her uninvolvement, which was her contribution to the family loyalty. Each one worked loyally to maintain the family system and the homeostasis.

5. **How well the members engage in loyal behaviors, and how well homeostasis is maintained, creates a specific, although perhaps unconscious and unspoken, definition for *success* in this particular family.**

An example of this is the family of bank robbers I referred to earlier. Their "success" was predicated not only on their ability to rob banks and get away with it, but also on their ability to keep all of the family members involved in the "bank-robbing" process.

Those particular points bring to mind a conversation I had with a professor during my doctoral program in California. We were having tea between classes at a little shop in Berkeley and discussing the information that our clients brought into therapy that they were convinced were universal truths. Her reply startled me somewhat. "David," she said, "I don't believe in truth anymore…only in function. Because people make up their own truths all the time." It was the *human* element of truth she was referring to—our ability and propensity as human beings to create convenient "truths" to meet our needs at any given point in time. And while there is *truth* in the universe—God's truth which is constant and inerrant, in our quest to be "right" in what we think or do, we have gotten into a habit of *creating* truth.

This one conversation triggered many more in which another important concept took form:

Behavior is functional

What this refers to specifically is what we addressed in the prologue of this book: *"nobody does nothin' for nothin,"* and that all of our behaviors have a meaning and purpose for us, and are perceived by us to have an important role in the family system.

During the years I lived in California, I developed a close relationship with a man who was an excellent golfer. And it was much to my benefit to be in that relationship because when we played golf together he also was a tireless and kind teacher. Never one to interfere with my mediocre golf game, he always waited until I asked for assistance and graciously (with a high degree of humor) took the time to tutor me in the finer points of the game. For example: "The driver is not a baseball bat, and if you continue to hold it like one, you will probably have less than desirable success."

And then he would take the time to show me the alternatives. It was a fun and fulfilling relationship.

One day he called *me* for assistance.

My friend had a son named Gary. Gary was in his senior year of high school and was a very bright, outgoing, and athletic young man. When I asked how I could help, my friend shared this story with me. It seems Gary, an extremely talented golfer in his own right, was having a great deal of difficulty at school and at home. Usually a very respectful kid (as teenagers go) he was belligerent and defiant with his parents, resisted going to church with them, did not come home on time, did not let them know where he was going—all things that had never been much of a problem to this point. In school his grades had dropped substantially, he had been caught skipping classes, and was at risk of being academically ineligible for the golf team, his only sport.

His father was beside himself. "We've done everything," he lamented. "We've talked and talked, we've threatened, tried bribery, asked 'why?' and all we get is, 'I don't know' and then silence. If he doesn't get a handle on this, he's going to risk losing his chance to make the All-State Golf Team this year."

I asked when this behavior had started and after checking with his wife they both agreed it had started around the time golf season had begun. I asked if there was any evidence of drug or alcohol use, or a change in his circle of friends, or any of the other things a therapist looks for to indicate substance abuse, because at first glance it seemed that the sudden change in behavior might have been related. Neither parent felt there was any indication of drug usage. I then asked how I might help. "I want you to see him professionally," my friend said. "He said he would go for counseling because he doesn't understand it either and he's miserable. But, he also said the only one he would go see was you." I shared with my friend that I felt uncomfortable with the professional relationship because of our personal relationship and suggested that perhaps we could keep it a bit more informal. Why not play golf together?

Two days later the three of us got together at the local country club and after meeting in the clubhouse for an early morning cup of coffee, we headed out to the first tee. As we moved through the first nine holes, I observed two excellent golfers showing their skill. The son was rather quiet, but the father was very vocal. It seemed with every shot that didn't go exactly the way he wanted, he berated himself—not greatly, but noticeably. This was a trait I had not seen when he and I played together.

"I should have used an 8-iron."

"I never should have tried to clear those trees."

"I really shanked that one."

And with each comment, *I watched the son watch the father.*

Meanwhile, the son was playing excellent golf, and being regularly complimented and cheered on by his father. When the son did make an error, the father would smile, and lovingly and appropriately share with him some alternatives and suggestions for how he might handle it differently next time.

And with each comment, *I watched the son watch the father.*

After the first nine holes the son was actually ahead of the father by three strokes, and we went into the clubhouse for a Coke. While we sat at a table together, the father went over his scorecard and commented on all of the things he should have done differently at each hole. He was experiencing a bad case of, "If only I had..."

And with each comment, *I watched the son watch the father.*

We finished our drinks and headed out toward the tenth tee. And there, without warning, I watched Gary fall apart. He began making poor choices that a novice like myself might make, not an accomplished golfer—even a young one. He was making poor club selections, taking unnecessary risks, his swing deteriorated right before our eyes, his follow-through was poor. To each one of those errors it would have been very easy to tell Gary, "Come on! You know better. What are you doing?" But his father did none of that. With each error, the father shared his perception of what had happened, and in very appropriate ways, instructed his son.

And with each comment, *I watched the son watch the father.*

Meanwhile, the father's game had not gotten any better, but he was certainly doing better than his son. By the time we were finished with our round of golf, the father had bested his son by three strokes, which means that Gary dropped six strokes on the back nine holes. They spent some time in practice and instruction, again, with the father teaching the son in very loving and helpful ways.

And with each comment, *I watched the son watch the father.*

And they were both happy.

We had some lunch together and talked lightly. I shared with Gary that I understood he was going through some "stuff," and that we could talk any time he wanted to. I prayed with my friends, and we parted.

Two days later my friend called me up and jovially asked, "So, Doc, what did you get out of our therapeutic golf game?" I took a deep breath and told him, "I will tell you what I saw. That's all I can do. What I saw was a very loyal young man who is sacrificing himself because he believes there is an unconscious and unspoken rule in this family that says, *"it's not okay to do better than dad, because dad's ego can't handle it."* Whether or not that rule has any basis in your reality is not important. Gary believes it is true, and out of his love and devotion removes himself from competition with you, directly and indirectly. What he needs from you, and doesn't have, is permission to be a better golfer than you are."

By the time I finished sharing my perceptions, my friend was crying on the other end of the phone. He knew what I was saying was true. He then shared with me that his family had been exposed all of their lives to his disappointment that he hadn't gone pro, that he hadn't had the self-esteem to pursue his dreams. And he also knew that the push for Gary's golf game was an attempt to live vicariously through his son, who he truly believed to be a gifted athlete. But, without permission, the son would never excel.

I met one time with Gary and his father and heard my friend explain to his son what had been happening, and his understanding of Gary's loyalty. He was able to give his son *overt* permission to be the best golfer he could be, and committed not only to be supportive of him, but also hold him accountable if he felt that Gary was being inappropriately loyal to the mistaken perception that it was not okay to do better than dad. He also asked his son's forgiveness for anything he had done, consciously or not, to hold his son back. He got it.

Gary placed second in the state that year in golf.

Although the loyalties are forged out of a desire to maintain the homeostasis of the family, if unrecognized or unchecked they can have lasting negative effects that carry down through generations. I have always maintained that *awareness is 51% of the cure.* If we can continue to be aware of our loyalties to the current family system, or to our family of origin, we have an opportunity to be *selective* toward keeping those loyal behaviors which are healthy and helpful to who we choose to be, and eliminate or adjust the ones that perpetuate dysfunctional, inappropriate, and unhealthy behaviors within the family system.

As I am writing this particular chapter, I am sitting on the front porch of the "family" summer cottage on a small lake in mid-Michigan. The cottage was purchased by my parents and grandparents when I was three years old, and has now been in the family for 42 years. My grandparents have passed on, but my parents, and now my sisters and their families, continue to spend weeks during the summer at the lake house. As children, my sisters and I spent every summer up here, learning to swim and water-ski, growing up with the neighbors, picking wild blueberries in the woods, and fishing for perch, bluegills, and bass in the lake. We loved it here and looked forward to every day we could spend on the lake.

Every day, that is, except one.

There was one day every summer when my mother would invite the members of our church's Women's Missionary Society to the lake. My mother was the youngest of these women, and didn't, I felt, have much in common with them, so I could never figure out why this annual event occurred. And, although they were, in my mind, "nice old ladies," why did they have to interfere with my summer? On that particular day the "fogies" (as my sisters and I called them) had the run of the entire place. They got the porch swing, the paddle boat, the canoe, the row boat, the ski boat, the dock, the lawn chairs. It seemed to us that they got *everything*, and that we were relegated to taking walks in the woods and staying out of the way for the entire day (which resembled eternity in our minds).

I think I must have been 13 or 14 when, on one day when these ladies were at the cottage, my father surprised me. He asked me if I wanted to ski. Was I hearing him right? After all, the Women's Missionary Society was here—all over the dock, beach, and boats. Was he serious?

I grabbed my slalom ski and life vest while he prepared the boat and ski rope, and we took off. I was having a ball, and wanted it to last a long, long time, so I stayed out until I thought I would drop from exhaustion. Finally I signaled my father that I wanted to go in, and we headed back toward our beach. As we rounded that last corner I could see those ladies sitting in lawn chairs on the beach and the dock. And my adolescent mind began to work. Now, any of you who water ski know that the delight of a slalom skier, when coming into shore, is to cut across the wake of the boat, pick up a lot of speed before letting go of the rope, racing toward shore, and sending up a huge wall of spray while stopping.

And I began to think…

"Should I? or Shouldn't I?"

Meanwhile, I'm noticing two other things are happening. My father is bringing me in faster than he typically does, and he is bringing me in closer than he usually does. So… at the last minute I decide.

"I should…"

Now, my mother, who was standing on the beach, knew what was about to happen. Her eyes got as wide as hubcaps, she opened her mouth to warn the ladies, and she tried to wave me off… but it was too late. I came screaming across that wake, let go of the rope, headed straight toward the dock and the beach, and, at the last possible moment, kicked back and sent up a wall of water that made significant contact with at least two-thirds of those ladies.

My mother was *hot!*

She went back and forth between yelling at me and consoling these women who were trying to figure out what just happened. Finally, she finished her tirade toward me with the vow, "I'll deal with you *later!*" and focused her attention on her guests. And as I quietly and nervously stood there on the beach, soaking wet with my ski in my hand, my father *slowly* pulled the boat into the dock and *slowly* wound up the ski rope and stowed it. He then walked up to me, and as we had our backs to the group of women on the beach drying off, he put his arm around my shoulder, looked down at me and *smiled,* and said,

"You know I'm going to have to ground you for that, don't you?"

And I said, "I know."

And we walked back up the hill to the cottage. Although I had no way of knowing it at the time, and doubt that my father consciously recognized it while it was occurring, my antic had created as much satisfaction for him as it did for me. My behavior had tapped into the mischievous part of him that he could not openly express. He later confessed that during these annual visits he was as bored as we kids were, and was looking for ways to entertain himself. My loyalty to him accomplished this task.

While some acts of family loyalty have short-term impact on the family and individuals involved (I think all of those ladies have forgiven me in the 30 years that have passed), there are other acts of loyalty that can have debilitating and devastating effects on the family system for generations. And if the pathology in the family is firmly entrenched, often the children involved will give in to the pressure to be loyal in ways that have a critical and negative effect on them.

An example of this type of loyalty can be seen in the issue of anorexia nervosa, an eating disorder where the subject, usually an early adolescent girl, eats only minimal amounts of food, becomes obsessed with her body image, considering any image of herself she sees reflected in the mirror to be "fat." And while we are most familiar with anorexia within the context of social pressures to look a certain way among adolescent girls (since society and the media perpetuate an unrealistic goal of thinness for most girls), there is another factor in anorexia that is all too often overlooked—family loyalty.

A 15-year-old girl named Ann was referred to me by her family physician for treatment of a long-standing eating disorder that had been going on for a period of at least three years. The onset of the eating disorder was found to coincide with the end of a long and messy divorce between her parents when she was twelve, a nasty split which ultimately saw her father leave the state and marry another woman. She was left at home with her mother and 12-year-old sister.

Her mother was a very insecure woman in her early 30's, slightly over-weight, who had dropped out of school when she became pregnant with Ann. She had never worked outside the home, until the divorce, and was a rather plain-looking woman who was trying desperately to update herself to become more attractive to possible suitors. She read all the latest fashion magazines, spent a significant amount of money on clothes, and wore heavy makeup to hide the wrinkles she called "the after-effects of being married to a jerk." She was very honest about not wanting to be alone and lonely. She was actively pursuing serious relationships. She figured she had had about nine serious relationships since the divorce had taken place, seemed unable to keep a relationship going in a positive direction, and couldn't figure out why she kept attracting alcoholic men like her husband and her own father.

Ann's sister, Marie, was slightly pudgy for a 12-year-old, and bore a resemblance to her mother. She was very dependent on her mother, and did not like to do things with friends or engage in activities outside the home without the mother's presence.

Ann was a very attractive adolescent who dressed plainly and wore no makeup. In this way she did not fit the profile of the adolescent anorexic. She weighed 86 pounds. and was 5'7" tall. She did not seem overly con-cerned with body image, and just said she didn't feel like eating. She had very little social interaction, did relatively well in school, but was called an "underachiever" by her teachers and mother. She spent a lot of time at home while her mother and sister went out. Ann was significantly depressed.

Why the eating disorder existed at all, and what the foundation of the depression was, presented a formidable puzzle. She could talk about her parents' divorce as having been hard, but that her father's alcoholism and open affairs had been so difficult for the family she was actually glad he was gone and did not miss him all that much. She could express the fact that mom's going to work had placed an additional burden on her, but it was not over and above what she was willing to do to help the family.

One day, Ann came into the office and said,

"I had a dream last night. Do you believe in dreams?"

I told her that I believed dreams could have significance in an indi-vidual's life, and asked her to tell me her dream.

"I saw this room and it seemed there was a party going on. My mother was there and my sister was there. I wasn't there, at first. There was music, and bright lights, and everyone was having lots of fun. I looked at my mother and didn't recognize her at first. She looked younger and very beautiful. And she was thin. Very thin. There were lots of men around her—talking to her. And she was very happy. My sister was there, too. She had lots of friends and they were singing to the music. No one noticed me or paid attention to me at all. Then I saw that this wasn't a party at all—it was a funeral. There was a casket in the corner of the room and lots of flowers. But I couldn't understand why everyone was so happy if this was a funeral. I walked over to the casket. The cover was shut. I lifted up the lid of the casket and saw me inside. It was horrible. It was like they were all so happy I was gone. Then I woke up. Does it mean anything?"

It did...

Subsequent meetings with Ann, Marie, and the mother revealed that there was a significant amount of jealousy on the part of the mother toward Ann who was younger, prettier, more vivacious, had boys who pursued her, and had far more opportunities ahead of her than the mother felt *she* had. In fact, it was Ann's birth that cut short her mother's *perceived potential*, what she felt she *would have accomplished* had she not gotten pregnant. This jealousy came out in the form of snide comments about Ann's weight, comments referring to the fact that the mother would have better luck with men if she didn't have the children to contend with. Ann was compared to her father (and she did, in fact, bear a striking resemblance to him), and told that she would probably "disappear" just like he did.

That was exactly what she was trying to do.

Ann knew her mother's self-esteem was low, and that she had a very hard time being around anyone who was younger, prettier, or had more opportunities than she. And Ann was ultimately able to talk about those feelings. "I knew my mom could be happier if I wasn't around. I really love her, but I guess I thought that if I could just disappear, then she would be able to be happy." So she became thinner...

and thinner...

and thinner...

What is the ultimate disappearing act? Death. And death would have been the ultimate act of loyalty on Ann's part toward her mother. Making the process overt for all of them helped the mother find healthy ways to enhance her own self-esteem not at the expense of her children. It also helped Ann emotionally detach from her mother's pathology and develop a life based on *her* needs, apart from the needs of the family system, and create new boundaries to ensure that when she *did* pursue ways to meet her mother's needs, it was not at her own expense or emotional/physical deficit.

Even Marie played a part in all of this. It was a true team effort. Marie attempted to look as much like her mother as possible and align herself with everything the mother did in an effort not to cross the boundaries of homeostasis her mother had set up. In order to accomplish this, she had to forgo social relationships outside the family and concentrate on the relationship with the mother alone. Her isolation made her insecure, and therefore more dependent on the mother. Through treatment, her mother helped her develop new friendships and presented her with opportunities outside the home to develop interests and relationships, allowing her to separate in healthy ways from the mother. With her mother's support there was a marked improvement in self-esteem, significant weight loss, and new friendships that she had always desired, but never had developed.

The mother was able to reflect on her own family of origin, on the alcoholic mother who abandoned the family, and the workaholic father who didn't have a clue about healthy families and reacted by spending more time at work. She was able to see how she had transferred her decision-making processes and family loyalties to her current situation, and how that had aided not only in the destruction of her marriage, but in the dysfunctional loyalty of her children. She could now begin to make different choices—healthy ones for herself and her daughters.

In this chapter we have seen that the inherent family loyalties within the family system can be negative or positive. They can, at times, be comical and ultimately insignificant in the lives of the individuals involved. Or, they can be excruciating and debilitating, sometimes irreparably damaging the parties unconsciously involved in doing their part to maintain the expected level of functioning within the family. We also have seen that often these acts of loyalty are predicated upon a *perception* that a family member may have regarding what is required or being asked of them in the family, whether or not that perception has any basis in reality. And that loyalty in a family system is a team effort which requires the distinct cooperation of *all* of the parties involved in order to make it work and maintain homeostasis. Our awareness of these dynamics will allow us to scrutinize how *we* are impacted as a result of our own family loyalties.

In the next chapter we will examine exactly how these loyalties cross generational boundaries in the form of messages we received—and our parents received—and their parents received—and their parents received...

Shadowchaser

THINK ABOUT YOUR OWN "FAMILY SCULPTURE." DESCRIBE IT BRIEFLY, REMEMBERING TO INCLUDE THINGS LIKE MATERIAL (GLASS, SAND, BRONZE, STEEL, ETC.), TEXTURE (SLIPPERY, ROUGH, PRICKLY, WET, SMOOTH, ETC.), TEMPERATURE (HOT, COLD, TEPID, FROZEN, ETC.), THE POSITION EVERYONE IS IN, THEIR MOTIONS AND EXPRESSIONS, AND ANYTHING ELSE YOU CAN THINK OF.

WHAT DOES THIS SCULPTURE REPRESENT TO YOU?

WHAT FEELINGS AND EMOTIONS DOES EXAMINING THIS SCULPTURE TRIGGER IN YOU RIGHT NOW?

IS THIS A COMMON FEELING FOR YOU, OR ONE THAT DOES NOT EMERGE VERY OFTEN?

WHAT "ACTS OF LOYALTY" CAN YOU REMEMBER COMMITTING IN YOUR FAMILY?

HAVE YOU CONTINUED ANY OF THOSE "LOYALTIES" SINCE LEAVING YOUR FAMILY OF ORIGIN?

CHAPTER 3

Gramma's Logic: A Primer

*"Only be careful, and watch yourselves closely
so that you do not forget the things your eyes have seen,
or let them slip from your heart as long as you live.
Teach them to your children and to their children after them.."*
–Deuteronomy. 4:9 NIV

*"The reason parents no longer lead their children
in the right direction is because the parents
aren't going that way themselves."*
–Frank McKinney Hibbard

There is a rather comical story about ham. It seems that a young girl was watching her mother prepare the Sunday meal before they left for church in the morning. The girl watched as her mother took the ham, sliced a portion off both ends, then put the ham into a pan, and, finally, into the oven.

"Why did you do that?" the young girl asked.

"Why did I do what?"

The mother looked quizzically at the daughter.

"Why did you cut off both ends of the ham, before you put it in the pan, before you put it in the oven?"

The mother's face clouded momentarily, considering her answer carefully before she finally said,

"I don't know. I guess it's because my mother did it."

The grandmother had been invited over for dinner, and during the meal the girl was reminded of her earlier question. "Gramma," she asked, "Why did you cut off both ends of the ham before you put it in the pan, before you put it in the oven?"

The grandmother thought for a few moments and then responded, "I don't know. I guess it's because my mother did it."

At this point curiosity got the best of all of them, and a call was put in to great-gramma who was living in a nursing home. "Great-Gramma," asked the girl, after explaining the situation, "why did you cut off both ends of the ham before you put it into the pan, before you put it into the oven." The great-grandmother laughed and without hesitation replied,

"That's an easy one. I only had one pan. That's the only way it would fit!"

In her situation the behavior was "functional" and had a very important purpose. She was limited in her utensils, and resourceful in her process, making do with what she had. However, that behavior had been carried for two successive generations, without question, long past the point of its original function. It was no longer necessary to continue cutting off the ends of the ham—but *habit* perpetuated the behavior. Had the little girl not questioned the procedure, it could have been carried through her generation as well.

Throughout our lives we tend to act and react according to a specific set of messages that we received throughout our lives. Most of these messages come from our parents or some other source extremely close to us, and *highly influential* in our lives. The messages that they received had been passed down to them from their parents or some source very important to them, and so on, down through the generations. These messages are instrumental in determining the choices we make in our lives. However, very often we act out on the messages as though we are on auto-pilot, accepting by rote the processes that those messages entail, never questioning their applicability to our own lives, desires, needs, or goals at any given point in our life cycle.

In 1981 my wife Colette (who also is a family therapist) and I were searching for a device which would help us to help others become more *conscious* of the motivating factors and messages in their lives. Unable to find a suitable tool at that time, we created the *Beighley Issues Awareness Scale (BIAS)*, a device designed to challenge individuals, couples, and families to examine the messages they had received from their families of origin, who the sender of that message was, and how they were (or were not) acting out on the messages they had received. It also helped them determine whether or not a message had specific healthy applicability to their lives at this time, or had an unhealthy impact on them and needed to be eliminated. We revised the scale in 1992 and it became the BIAS-R. The Shadowchaser at the end of this chapter includes the BIAS-R. Go there now and complete the exercise (this exercise is duplicated in the *Dancing with*

Yesterday's Shadows workbook if you would prefer not to write your answers in the spaces provided). What you discover there will help you put the information contained in the rest of this chapter into a more "up close and personal" perspective. The instructions are simple, but the process is often difficult, and mentally/emotionally challenging. I will follow the BIAS-R with examples of messages I have encountered in clinical practice, and how those messages impacted the individual and their current family system.

Let's go exploring!

By examining your answers in the BIAS-R, you will quickly discover several things. First, that some issues were more important in your family of origin than others. Second, that some of the issues were more emotionally charged for you than others. And, third, that some of the issues are having a great impact on you, either positively or negatively, in your current relationships. Let's examine some of the messages that individuals have received and look at the resulting impact from that conscious or unconscious exchange.

There are three issues which seem to come up in therapy more often than any others: *Money, Sex, and Children.*

The first home I remember living in was a small green stucco house on a very busy street. It had a large back yard and our neighbor grew rhubarb in a small garden next to our yard. He had a fence around it with openings just large enough for me to get my hand through, and often I did. It is this scenario that I picture when I consider the issue of *money.* I can recall being in that house on the first and the fifteenth of each month—payday for my parents who both worked outside the home. And I can recall them, after dinner was done and the dishes cleared, sitting at the white with gray-flecked Formica table in the high-backed green and blue floral print chairs. A small hanging lamp shone overhead as they pored over the bills spread out in front of them. As I picture that scene, I can hear my mother's voice saying, about money, "It seems no matter how much we have, there's never quite enough to pay all the bills." They were a young couple, new homeowners struggling to make ends meet during this stage of their relationship. And the message I received from them during that time was consistent.

And I internalized it.

I was one of those kids for whom money burned a hole in my pocket. If I had a nickel, I tried to spend a dime. If I earned a dollar, I tried to find a way to spend five dollars. And this continued as I grew older. I *looked* for ways to spend money, even when I didn't have any. I would make a purchase that would strap me, and shortly after I did it would ask, "Why on earth did I do that?" My personal fiscal follies continued into college and marriage. At one point, after I was married and in graduate school, my wife found a job that necessitated our buying a second car. We saved, and saved, and saved (no small task for me) until we had accumulated $2,500. And it was going to be my job to shop and find a suitable vehicle for us. On the appointed day I set out to see how best we could utilize our finances to purchase that second vehicle, and I did just that. In a matter of hours I had returned home with a Corvette! Our $2,500 had made a *wonderful* down payment on such a great vehicle. And, I got *such* a good deal.

And as I'm driving home I am experiencing a myriad of thoughts.

"Wow, what a great car."

"She's going to kill me."

"Why did I do this to myself again?"

"This is really going to strap us for cash."

"You'd think I'd learn my lesson somewhere along the line."

And, I was right on all accounts. It wasn't until several years later that I was able to determine that my behaviors were linked to the message about money that was most predominant in my unconscious thought processes—that no matter how much there was, for me there was never going to be quite enough. I was going to see to it. However, it is extremely important to note *that the message I received was in no way the message my parents were attempting to send me.* My parents were and are an extremely fiscally responsible couple. They always paid their bills, and made consistently wise and informed choices in purchases and investments. They are retired now and having the time of their lives as a result of the way they handled their finances. How did I, then, go awry? Herein lies an important concept regarding messages and the children who receive them.

Children are excellent observers but horrible interpreters

I am reminded of an instance when Nicholas was about three years old, and, like most normal three-year-olds, was determined to handle a certain situation his own way. Colette turned to him and said, "Nicholas, you are acting *very naughty!*" Nicholas became immediately indignant in a way that only three-year-olds can manage, looked at Colette, and said,

*"Mommy, I am **not** acting!"*

Because children process information differently than adults, there is always the possibility that the message sent by the parents is not the same as the message that the child received. And even if the message is "heard" correctly, there is no guarantee that the child conceptually understands the behavioral dynamics of that message.

A family in our church, who happen to live up the road from us, underwent a tremendous tragedy this past year when both parents developed cancer and died within two months of one another, leaving two mid-adolescent boys. The boys then moved away to live with an older step-sister. As we were trying to explain the situation to Nicholas and Chloë, Nicholas asked,

"What would happen to us if you died?"

"Well, mommy and daddy have made arrangements that you would go live with Aunt Peggy and Uncle Chuck."

He thought for a moment and then slowly said, "Okay...does that mean I would take Chloë by the hand and walk over to their house?"

Our hearts just broke! We assured him that he would not have to do that, and that there would be many, many adults who would make sure he and Chloë were okay and taken care of.

But, all Nicholas was doing was trying to make sense of the situation as he was able to conceptualize it in *his* mind. And it was a reminder to us that we had to explain, as best we could, on his level to help him understand how things work.

Later we will address the importance of checking in with our children to ascertain whether or not they are accurately receiving the messages we send them. But for now, we need to evaluate the possibility that messages our parents sent us regarding important issues in our lives are the same messages we heard, interpreted, and internalized. This is important because of the need to be personally responsible and accountable for our behaviors, and not play the "blame game" with our parents. Author and lecturer Leo F. Buscaglia, made this statement in one of his lectures: "People tell me all the time, 'My parents did this to me,' or 'My parents did that to me.' I'll tell you what your parents did to you—they did the best job they knew how. That's what they did to you. *No parent, unless they are psychotic, has ever set out to hurt their child.*"

And while I believe that his statement is inherently true, our task is to evaluate what our perceptions of the messages were, and make decisions about how we want to incorporate them, adjust them, or eliminate them from our lives *now*.

Let's examine some of the other common messages individuals receive about the issue of money:

"If you've got it—spend it."

"Never spend for pleasure until *all* the bills are paid."

"If you can't pay cash for it—don't buy it."

"Never go into debt."

"If deficit spending is good enough for the government, it's good enough for me."

"If there are checks in the checkbook, I've got money to spend."

"If you don't have cash, there's always plastic."

"Make sure you save for a rainy day."

"Neither a lender nor a borrower be."

What messages did *you* receive about this important issue, and how, through the years have you processed the message in a way that it creates healthy behaviors and responses from you?

In my role as a minister, I had the pleasure of performing a marriage for a young couple several years ago. They had gone through the premarital counseling classes that our clinic offers and had also gone through individual counseling with me. I felt confident that we had covered most of the essential elements of a premarital evaluation before the wedding day. Their wedding was a very nice one, and they exchanged the personal vows they had written that were very meaningful to them. And, then, away they went on their honeymoon.

I didn't hear from the couple for about six months, until I got a panicked phone call from the husband. "You've got to see us right away," he insisted, "Our marriage is falling apart, and I don't know what to do about it." I scheduled an appointment for them in my earliest opening, wondering what could have gone so wrong so quickly in their young marriage.

On the day of the appointment he couldn't wait to get into my office and start talking. "It's this *sex* thing, Doc. Something is very, very wrong, and I know it's me. She wants to have sex, and please me and stuff, and she's very open about sex, but I have a big problem. *I don't like it!* It doesn't feel right to me, and when we have sex I feel like I've done something wrong, or that someone is watching me and I'm going to get into trouble. I just don't get it. I thought this was supposed to be really wonderful stuff."

I had a reasonable belief from our premarital counseling that he was inexperienced sexually when they got married, and wondered if it could be his inexperience that was creating the most difficulty. But evaluation of that line of thinking turned up nothing concrete. I then asked him to think about the messages he had gotten regarding sexuality from his family of origin, and explained to him the concept of the BIAS. He was the youngest child of three, and the only boy. His oldest sister had gotten pregnant in high school and the family experienced quite a bit of shame regarding the experience. His mother had been sexually molested in her family of origin and had gotten pregnant as a result. She opted for an abortion at that time, and had been in therapy for several years working through those issues. His father, a member of the church board, had been having an affair for several years that the son accidentally found out about just prior to getting married. He wanted to confront his father with the knowledge, but didn't know how. He related these facts to me as he sat in the office pondering the messages he had received. Then, a knowing look crossed his face and he said, "Now I understand. I got a real mixed message regarding sexuality from my parents. From my mother, who had been abused, and then had to handle my sister's pregnancy, I got a very clear and verbal message about sex: *don't.* From my father I got a very different message, this one nonverbal, and I'm sure he would not even admit to sending me this message. But the message from him was, *don't get caught.* So the two most significant messages I received about sex were both extremely negative and antagonistic. No wonder it doesn't feel right or good to me. I never stood a chance!"

Armed with that new information, he and his wife were able to write some new messages and create some new healthy sexual attitudes and behaviors. But, even with the new information, the transition was not an easy one. Remember homeostasis? If he was to enjoy the experience of healthy sexuality with his bride, that would be a conscious act of *disloyalty* to his family, and he would feel that emotionally. It was necessary for him to acknowledge over and over and over again that he *was* committing an act of family disloyalty, and that this disloyalty was healthy for him and his wife.

Very often changing the messages we received does not *feel* right to us because of the disloyalty. It is important to acknowledge that the anxiety we feel over not being loyal does not necessarily mean that the decision to change the message was a bad one. It simply means that it is *different* from the homeostatic way of functioning we experienced earlier in our lives and that and it will take some "getting used to."

Some other messages commonly received regarding sex are:
"Sex is dirty."
"Sex is a very wonderful thing with the right person."
"Sex is only for procreation."
"Only whores and tramps enjoy sex."
"Sex is to be reserved for marriage, and then it is fine."
"If it feels good—do it."

"Your body is dirty—don't share it with anyone."
"Sex is something great to be shared between two people."
"Don't get pregnant/AIDS/protect yourself."

The messages we have received about sex will dictate our sexual relationships if left on the unconscious level. Making the internal, covert messages open and conscious will allow us to evaluate the messages and create new ones that fit the person we choose to be sexually.

The issue of children raises all sorts of pictures and messages including the ones you received about being a child, the ones you received about children in general, and the ones you project on your children. Unlike many of the messages we receive, our behavioral manifestations of the messages regarding children don't necessarily appear until we ourselves have children and find ourselves treating those children in ways we vowed would never happen. Do you remember saying, either to yourself or to your parents after some less than desirable encounter, "I'll never treat my kids that way," or "My kids will never have to go to bed this early/eat spinach/take a bath three times a week, etc." And then we have children and find ourselves sending them to bed early, making them eat spinach, and bathe regularly. The concept goes right back to homeostasis, function, and all too often the "comfort in pain" lesson I learned from Leroy (Chapter 1). As parents, we tend to parent like our parents, at least initially. We do this for no other reason than that's what we know, that's what we experienced, and those behaviors correspond with what we have grown comfortable with. Remember—that can also mean "uncomfortably comfortable."

Jesse was seven years old when his parents brought him in for counseling. It wasn't so much counseling that they wanted. They were looking for someone to *"fix this kid before one of us kills him."* While the parents described a child who ran the family, threw temper tantrums at will, set his own meal and bed schedule, and wreaked general havoc around the house, Jesse was under his chair, behind his chair, examining my walking stick collection, pulling leaves off the plants, rummaging through his mother's purse, and untying his father's shoes. The two most common phrases heard in my office that evening were, *"No,* Jesse!" and "Stop it, Jesse!" Finally I asked Jesse to sit in his seat so I could talk to him. "You are the most powerful seven-year-old I have met in my whole life," I told Jesse. "It seems that you get to do whatever you want. Tell me how you got to be so powerful." Jesse looked up at me with a determined look in his eye and said, "It's easy. My mom and dad will say *no* six times." "And then what?" I asked with a certain degree of amusement. "Then," said Jesse, "they'll say *yes.*" And with a sideways glance toward his parents I told him, "Jesse, as long as that keeps working, you keep doing it."

The last message was not directed so much at Jesse as it was to his parents. Both were very inconsistent with Jesse and were sending him a behavioral message: "Ultimately you can wear us down and you'll get your way." Both parents came from homes where the parents disciplined by screaming, and they vowed they would be more tolerant and not scream. However, they didn't know *how* to discipline effectively with more tolerance, so when Jesse began wearing them down they ended up screaming at him and then giving in. It was necessary for the parents to do more than vow they would not parent like their parents did. It was also necessary for them to learn *new* and effective methods of parenting their child.

Some of the common messages regarding children that people carry with them are:
"Children are to be seen, and not heard."
"You're just a kid. You don't know anything."
"You'll never amount to much."
"When will you ever learn?"
"Are you dense or something?"
"You are a really special person."
"I'm so glad God gave you to me to take care of."
"You are my princess/prince."
"You gave it your best shot. That's what counts."

It is in the area of parenting that the messages we have received and that we send to our children have potentially crossed over more generational levels than in any other issue. And it is in this area where our definitions of what a "man" is and what a "woman" is are founded. We begin to formulate ideas about what is expected of us gender-wise, and these messages come not only from what we experience as directed toward us, but what gender roles we see our parents playing out in their marriages.

Early in my career I spent three years in the military working for the Department of Psychology and Psychiatry at Reynolds Army Hospital, Ft. Sill, Oklahoma. One Friday afternoon, shortly before we were going to leave for the weekend, a "walk-in" appeared in the office. This was an individual who did not have an appointment, but could come in and be seen by anyone who happened to be available at the time. On that particular day I was available. She filled out the paperwork and the secretary brought it back to my office. On that paperwork I read about a 19-year-old woman from Tennessee who was married to an infantryman and going through "marriage problems and communication problems." When I went to the waiting room and called her name, I was confronted with a tall, thin woman, rather unkempt, wearing shorts, a halter top, and sandals. But, it wasn't her outfit that was the most striking thing about her. It was the large number of bruises, some fresh and some fading, that covered most of the visible parts of her body. When she got back to my office I asked, "What happened to you?" She looked puzzled at first, but then saw me looking at her bruises. "Oh, those," she said with a shrug. "My husband beat me up a little bit." She said this with such nonchalance that it made the hair on the back of my neck stand up. "How often does that happen?" I asked. She shrugged again, and, looking out my office window, calmly stated, *"I guess no more often than the average husband beats up his wife."*

You see, she had come from a family where if the mother was not performing up to the father's standards, he beat her up. And her husband had come from a family where if the mother was not doing as the father desired or expected, he beat her up. She had come to expect that this was part of her calling as a woman, and that if she was going to be married, she was going to be beat up. And while she had heard that not every husband beat up his wife, and that the physical abuse was unacceptable, this was not her *experience* either as an observing daughter or a participating wife. Therefore she chose not to accept any other reality. She soon dropped out of treatment and returned home to what she knew best.

By the same token, the inverse is also true. When I observe healthy couples, treating one another with respect and honor, I have a certainty regarding what they learned about themselves as individuals. They learned they had worth, value, and the ability to be competent apart from one another that allowed them to engage in a healthy relationship *with* one another. As Colette and I travel throughout the country, we have the opportunity to observe what we consider to be healthy couples and families in a business and social setting. When we have the opportunity to discuss with some of these individuals the things in their backgrounds that had the most influence on them, we find that they *consistently* received positive, healthy messages that were reinforced by positive behaviors in their families of origin. In the next chapter we'll discuss more about how that happens and what is required to sustain it over time.

Perhaps the one other area in which multigenerational messages have their greatest and most resolute impact is within the issue of *success*. Success is first and foremost defined within the multigenerational family of origin, typically at least through two previous generations, then in the nuclear family, and then from outside sources (who have the least impact on the working definition). Each family seems to have its own "invisible ceiling" of success—that level of competency past which the individuals choose, out of loyalty, to not exceed. The ceiling creates a comfort level within the family system that "we're all on the same level here, speaking the same language, and doing the same things." In order to maintain that level of "success" in the family, members "at risk" for exceeding the prescribed levels of success are often discouraged, undermined, or diverted.

Janice came from a family in which her grandmother on her father's side was the only one of the family who had ever gone to college. The grandmother's husband was a blue-collar worker who divorced her after the fifth of five children was born, and abandoned the family, never to be seen again. This grandmother had gone on to be a teacher and had retired after a successful teaching career. The rest of the extended family was made up of blue-collar workers, individuals on public assistance, and many members who struggled with drug and alcohol abuse. When my friend made the decision to go to college the feedback she got was as follows:

"Why would you want to do anything like that?"

"You'll never amount to anything anyway."

"You should just get married. You could find someone to take care of you."

"Why start what you'll never finish?"

In therapy Janice learned that she was not going to be able to rely on her nuclear or extended family to give her financial or emotional support for her journey, and that if she was going to redefine what success meant to her, she was also going to have to create some distance between herself and her family. She did that, believing that once she finished her degree, the family would see that she *did* do it, and be happy for her and accepting of her. Her experience, however, upon finishing her degree was that she was greeted with suspicion and hostility. Now it was, "Who does she think she is? Miss Smarty Pants?" Janice had violated the boundaries of success set forth by the family. Her statement to me was, "I got my degree, but lost my family in the process." Many times, redefining your specific and behavioral criteria for success will be an overt act of disloyalty to the family, and rejection will often follow.

Typical messages regarding success include the following:

"You can do anything you want. Go for it."

"You'll be a failure just like your father."

"Don't worry, we never did very well in school either."

"Just get by, it'll be okay."

"The sky's the limit."

"You've got to push for all you're worth—then you'll succeed."

"I want more for you than I ever had. Go after it."

"Don't be afraid to dream big dreams. Then make it happen."

It is through the consistent verbal *and* behavioral messages that we learned how to *be* in our families and in our lives, and it is through those same types of messages that we will teach our children. In this chapter you have been challenged to examine more carefully the messages that you received which have become the basis for your actions and reactions. It is out of that increased awareness that you will be able to determine whether or not the messages fit the person you want to become, and whether you want to hang on to them or trade them in for new messages that fit a new set of goals for yourself. It isn't anything anyone can tell you, it is something you "know." Perhaps it is best to follow the words of Antoine de St. Exeupery's *Little Prince,* "It is only with the heart that one sees rightly. What is essential is invisible to the eye." As you examine your history, your head, and your heart, prayerful consideration and scrutiny of the functions of your messages historically and in the present will create a road map to help you go in new directions.

You've got the map right in your hands. Let's move ahead on the journey.

THE BEIGHLEY ISSUES AWARENESS SCALE
Ψ
BEIGHLEY ISSUES AWARENESS SCALE-REVISED-© (BIAS-R©)

There are no "right" or "wrong" answers to these issues. Your answers will assist you in understanding how the messages you received as a result of growing up in your particular family of origin impact you in your life and relationships today.

On the following two pages are lists of issues. These are common issues in everyone's life, to some degree. Please look at each issue individually and consider this question: What is the *"message"* that I received regarding this issue, and where did it come from? Usually the sender is a parent, although it can be some other very influential individual in your life. The message may be verbal or behavioral, explicit or implicit, overt or covert. The message may be mixed—one message from one parent and another, perhaps conflicting, message from the other parent. For example, on the issue of *"money"*, a child might hear from one parent, "If you have it—spend it," and from the other parent, "No matter how much we have, there is never enough."

Do not think too long about any one issue. If you cannot decide on an answer, skip that issue and come back to it after you have finished the others. If a particular issue holds no relevance in your family of origin, mark NA in the Sender column and go on. There also are blank spaces at the end of the scale to insert issues which may have been important in your family of origin, but are not included on these lists.

ISSUE	SENDER	MESSAGE
Family		
Friends		
Home		
Manhood		
Womanhood		
Sex		
Joy		

Beighley Issues Awareness Scale© (BIAS-R©) Continued

ISSUE	SENDER	MESSAGE
Love		
God		
Church		
Money		
Success		
Faith		
Education		
Fear		
Failure		
Loyalty		
Pain		
Anger		
Secrets		
Play		
Emotion		
Work		
Intelligence		
Occupation		

Beighley Issues Awareness Scale© (BIAS-R©) Continued

ISSUE	SENDER	MESSAGE
Holidays		
Marriage		
Children		
Power		
Respect		
Death		
Wisdom		
Divorce		
Fighting		
Food		
Forgiveness		
Sin		
Shame		
Jokes		
Politics		
Honesty		
OTHER		
OTHER		

Shadowchaser

RANK THE TOP 10 ISSUES IN THE ORDER OF HOW
IMPORTANT THEY WERE IN YOUR FAMILY OF ORIGIN,
WITH "1" BEING THE MOST IMPORTANT.

DID YOUR ANSWERS TO ANY "MESSAGES" YOU RECEIVED
SURPRISE YOU? WHICH ONES?

GO BACK OVER THE MESSAGES AGAIN. PLACE A + NEXT
TO THE ONES YOU CONSIDER TO HAVE A POSITIVE IMPACT
ON YOUR LIFE TODAY. PLACE A - NEXT TO THE ONES YOU
CONSIDER TO HAVE A NEGATIVE IMPACT ON YOUR LIFE
TODAY. PLACE A "C" NEXT TO THE THREE MESSAGES YOU
WOULD LIKE TO BEGIN CHANGING IMMEDIATELY IN YOUR
LIFE.

WHAT BEHAVIORS DO YOU EXHIBIT AT THIS POINT IN
YOUR LIFE THAT REFLECT THE MESSAGES YOU WOULD
MOST LIKE TO CHANGE?

CHAPTER 4

When 1+1=3, 4, 5, or 6

*"For this reason a man will leave his father and mother
and be united to his wife, and they will become one flesh."*
–Genesis 2:24 NIV

*"The honeymoon is over when he phones
that he'll be late for supper—
and she has already left a note
that it's in the refrigerator."*
–Bill Lawrence

Tony and Jackie were in love when they got married. They were in *deep* love. They couldn't get enough of each other and spent every spare, waking moment with one another. Their marriage came at the end of an intense four-month courtship that was passionate and deep. They felt they knew everything there was to know about the other. They were *really* in love and ready to get married.

So, what was the problem?

Why was this couple so deeply in love calling for an appointment for marital therapy four months into their marriage?

Because they were making each other *crazy!*

One of the initial questions I ask any couple who comes into therapy is, "What was the event or events that precipitated calling for an appointment?" Most often there have been some things brewing just below the surface of a relationship, but there is typically one event that pushes the couple to say, "That's it! We need some help."   For Tony and Jackie it was a situation that occurred on their "date night" two weeks earlier. Tony had pulled some strings and gotten tickets to a concert that he and Jackie had been talking about for weeks. They were both really excited and looking forward to the event. Everything had been planned. They had both gotten off work early, the car had gas, Tony had stopped at the ATM for money—they were all set to go.

It's now fifteen minutes past the time they had agreed to leave. Tony is standing at the front door with his coat on and Jackie's coat over his arm and her purse in hand. He is pacing. He is yelling up the stairway toward their bedroom, "C'mon Jackie! What's the deal? You said you'd be ready. You always do this to me. What's your problem? You're going to screw this up, too!"

Meanwhile, Jackie is stepping out of the shower and reaching for a towel. "I'll be there in a few minutes. Stop screaming at me. Why are you always so hyper? You knew I had to take a shower. You always do this do me. You're going to ruin this for me if you don't stop. What's the big deal? We're only going to be a little late."

When a relationship is formed it brings *two* people together…or does it? A well known therapist once asked the question regarding marriage, "How many people are sleeping in *your* bed?" In every marriage there are a myriad of influences that come from previous relationships, family loyalties, and unresolved issues from the family of origin. These influences cannot help but have an impact on the marriage, and in many instances those influences will dictate why we chose to be in that particular relationship in the first place!

The Gruesome-Twosome

Tony and Jackie had one of the most common types of relationships that exist in marriages today—they were the *"Gruesome-Twosome."* The Gruesome-Twosome is the couple that can't live with each other—and can't live without each other. There is great love and passion in the relationship, but the dynamics of the relationship create great strife for the individuals *and* the couple. The relationship is based on two important factors: *differences* and *completion*. Let's examine Tony and Jackie's backgrounds in regard to two important issues in a marriage: *Time* and *Order*.

In regard to the issue of time, Tony grew up in a very strict and rigid home. In his family the message regarding time was, "If you're not ten minutes early, you're late. And there is *no* excuse for being late." In his home he had the "20 to 1" rule for curfew. He had a very specific curfew and for every minute he was late, he had to be in 20 minutes earlier the following time he went out. Tony recalled having been grounded many times for being late for supper, or a family outing. So, time was a very big factor in his family.

In regard to the issue of order, Tony describes his home this way, "I could have functioned perfectly well in my home if I had been blind. Everything had its place and everything had better be in its place! My parents liked consistency, and they ran their home that way." Tony's father was one of those men who had pegboard up in the garage, and had all of the tools outlined in black marker, so you could immediately tell where a specific tool went, or if one was missing. Order was also a very big factor in his family.

Things were *quite* different around Jackie's house. Jackie came from what some people might call a "laid-back" family. Others might term it "chaotic." Neither time nor order were all that important in this family. The "family rule" regarding time was somewhat of a joke both in and out of the family system, "If you're an hour either way, you're okay." It was not uncommon to hear the mother or father, when asked about the timing of something, reply, "We'll get there when we get there." Or, "It will happen when it happens!"

Tony recalls going to dinner at Jackie's house before they were married and offering to help with dishes after dinner. Having dried a platter, he asked Jackie's mom, "Where should I put this?" She gave him a puzzled look, smiled, shrugged, pointed at a cupboard and said, "Wherever there's room." In this household, car keys, checkbooks, school materials, and business papers were lost on a regular basis, and there was always a last minute, helter-skelter rush on the part of the family members to find something before they left the house. It was evident that time and order were not among the priorities of this family.

How then, out of all of the millions of people in the world, did Tony and Jackie get together? What was the attraction that would draw them toward one another despite such clear and drastic differences?

That's exactly what drew Tony and Jackie together—the *differences.* The old adage is true that opposites attract, but let's examine that principle and find out why it so often doesn't work. When Jackie became involved with Tony and got to know his family, her initial thought was, "Whew, *finally,* some structure in my life. After having grown up with all the chaos, this is great— a family that has some structure in it. At last, something I can depend on."

When Tony became involved with and got to know Jackie's family, his initial thought was, "Whew, *finally,* some laid-back people in my life. After having grown up with all that anal-retentive rigidity, this is great—a family that has some flexibility in it. At last, a place to relax."

Tony and Jackie were attracted to one another and to each other's families based on traits that the other had, that they each *did not* have. But, what they failed to realize is very important.

They didn't have those traits for a very important reason. They couldn't tolerate them!

It was the very things that had drawn them together that were making them crazy! Tony had not yet learned that if he wanted more flexibility in his life, he had to learn how to incorporate it into *his* life—to create it for himself. He had to learn to identify what the messages regarding time and order were in his family of origin, determine that these would not work for him, and be prepared to commit a conscious act of disloyalty (in healthy and appropriate ways) that would help him achieve flexibility. He couldn't get it from Jackie!

Jackie had not learned that if she wanted more structure in her life, she had to learn how to incorporate it into *her* life; to create it for herself. She also had to learn to figure out what messages she had received in her family of origin regarding structure, determine that these were not helpful to her at this point in her life, create a new message that would promote healthy interactions in her marriage, and be prepared to commit that same conscious act of disloyalty to the family of origin that would help her achieve structure. She couldn't get it from Tony. Both were looking to the other to *complete* them, provide for them a trait or traits that they themselves did not have. Both had to learn that *completion comes from within—not from without!*

The attraction of opposites can often be seen in the most important of issues in our relationships. You may witness it in the highly spiritual individual looking for someone to "save," and the non-spiritual individual looking for something significant in their life—looking to be "saved." Or, perhaps the highly responsible person who has developed into a caretaker who gravitates toward a more irresponsible individual who desires to be taken care of.

Shadowchaser

RECALL WITH YOUR MATE OR SIGNIFICANT OTHER THE EARLY STAGES OF YOUR RELATIONSHIP. ASK YOURSELVES THE QUESTION, "HOW, OUT OF ALL OF THE MILLIONS OF PEOPLE IN THE WORLD, DID WE GET TOGETHER?" WHAT WERE THE ATTRACTIONS? WERE THE MOST APPEALING CHARACTERISTICS OPPOSITE OF THE ONES YOU POSSESS? HOW HAS THAT ATTRACTION CHANGED OVER THE LENGTH OF THE RELATIONSHIP?

The Director-Director

We can see how the "opposites-attract" marriage stems from unresolved personal issues rooted in the family of origin, and that it has some built-in problems which can inhibit growth and success in that marriage. There is another common type of marriage that also has some potential road-blocks to growth and fulfillment, but this one is based on *similarities,* not differences. I call this one the *Director-Director* relationship.

In this relationship the personalities of the individuals involved tend to be very similar and very strong traits you might find in the Director on the set of a motion picture. However, on most movie sets, *there is only **one** Director!* In looking at their families of origin, we find that the personalities of their parents and siblings tended to be very strong as well. The similarities in their personalities tend to be content-based rather than process-based, and this is what tends to create the difficulties. Let's take a look at the potential conflicts created when *content* and *process* collide in the marriage of Frank and Ann.

Frank and Ann share similar views on almost every important issue in the relationship. They share the same spiritual views and beliefs in God. They agree on denominational preferences and what they desire in a church and church programming. These are *content* issues.

However, Ann doesn't "do" mornings and wants to go to the late service. Frank wants to attend the early service so they have the rest of the day to do family things. She thinks it's important to participate with the children and wants to teach a Sunday School class for preschoolers. He thinks it's important for them to learn and grow spiritually together, and wants both of them to attend the Adult Sunday School Class taught by one of the staff pastors. Frank wants to run for a position on the church's board of administration, which meets twice a month on Tuesday evenings, and Ann thinks he should devote his week time to her and the family when he is not working. These are *process* issues.

Because of the strength of their personalities, Frank and Ann argue passionately and intensely regarding the issues. Let's look at a few more content/process scenarios.

Both individuals agree that getting a full and dynamic education for their children is of paramount importance. They agree that ongoing contact with the school system, principal, and the teachers is very important. They mutually believe that a parent should not leave the child's education up to the school and teachers, but that they should supplement that education with other opportunities for the child to learn, like outside classes, family field trips, and additional workshops when available.

Ann wants to work in the classroom two days a week as a volunteer aide. Frank is afraid that her presence will be distracting to their child. He wants to run for the school board. She says he is overextending his time away from home and that she is afraid that will be at the expense of the family. Frank wants to take the children out of school for a business trip to Memphis for four days to show them the historical significance of a place they've never visited before. Ann wants to keep the children in their classroom and is afraid they would miss too much school. They can go to Memphis some other time.

They recently bought a home that required some fixing up to make it what they wanted it to be for their family. They both loved the house when they saw it. They thought the neighborhood was fantastic, and they liked the idea that they could stay in the same school system. Ann and Frank together compiled a list of changes they agreed would take place in the house and had researched the cost factors involved. They were in agreement on every one of these issues.

Frank felt that the hot tub was a far greater priority than new curtains because the hot tub was something that the whole family could use, and the old curtains were fine for right now. For him the curtains were "just an aesthetic thing." For Ann, *"Absolutely not!"* Ann insisted that Frank could use her father's table saw and sander, that he didn't need to go out and buy those tools in order to work on the house. They weren't "on the list." For Frank, *"Absolutely not!"* He needed his own tools if he was going to do the job right.

Both Frank and Ann felt that their sexual relationship was very important to the mutual satisfaction of each as individuals, and as a strengthener to the marriage. They were very open communicators regarding their sexuality and sexual relationship, had read many books about enhancing their sexual union, and were very sensitive and attentive to each other's sexual needs.

Frank has to get up at 5 a.m. in order to make the morning commute to work on time, and likes to be in bed between 10 and 11 p.m. Ann (who, remember, doesn't do mornings) feels that the evenings are her only time to unwind and relax after the kids go to bed, and likes to stay up to catch Leno and the news. Frank tends to run "hot" physiologically and typically goes to bed nude. He wishes Ann did also. Ann tends to run "cold" physiologically and often dresses in flannels and has her electric blanket turned on at least an hour before she goes to bed, and wishes he would understand that. Frank could make love anywhere and tells her about his fantasies of making love on a deserted beach sometime. "That sounds uncomfortable," she tells him. "What about the sand?"

It is the fact that they have so much in common from a content standpoint that a couple like Ann and Frank are initially attracted to one another. There are *strong common interests which create strong common bonds*. In this type of a relationship, it becomes essential when discussing *any* issue, to discuss that issue *not only from the content point of view, but simultaneously from the process point of view.* This is what creates a package of communication that will assist them in determining how things are going to work on the front end, to avoid the arguments and conflicts on the back end. The family of origin messages concerning mate selection and marriage were messages like:

> "Be sure to marry someone who agrees with you on the important issues (like I did)."

> "You're a strong personality, be sure you marry someone who can keep up with you."

> "Don't ever marry someone weak. You'll have to do all the work."

> "Just be sure you marry someone who agrees with you on the basics. The rest will work itself out."

The couple rarely received family-of-origin instruction regarding *how* to work things out, only on what to look for in terms of agreement. As the couple learns to become much more process-oriented, the arguing and negative interactions tend to diminish, and the passion and intensity can be reserved for problem-solving and bonding.

The Chaos Connection

The next type of relationship I want to examine is what I call the *Chaos Connection.* This type of a relationship has very intense connections to the family of origin and is one of the most destructive relationships in terms of the marriage as well as the impact on the children. Through the messages that the children receive about the processes of conflict resolution, it also sets them up to perpetuate the dysfunctional family system after they leave home and begin their own dysfunctional family.

Having learned no other alternatives, this marriage is based on arguing, yelling, screaming, fighting, throwing things, and often physical abuse as the primary form of communication. The marriage was based on the fact that the man and woman could "speak each other's language," a language of chaos and pain. It is what they grew up with all their lives, in their own families of origin, and they don't know any differently. As opposed to the Director-Director marriage, which is based on content at the expense of process, the Chaos Connection marriage is based on maintaining the same process (chaos) at the expense of the content. In this marriage, it really doesn't matter what the issue is. Every issue is settled (as opposed to resolved) in the same way. The parties go to war to see who is going to win. What they fail to realize is that in healthy coupleship, if any interaction does not culminate in a win-win scenario, the couple loses. There is quite often the additional factor of drug or alcohol abuse somewhere in this family history. The reason is simple. With drug or alcohol abuse there is a natural tendency to be unable to inhibit inappropriate behavior and be out of control much more easily. This makes the chaos much more easily attainable, understandable, and, unfortunately, excusable to the participants. "He (or she) wouldn't be that way if they weren't drinking." Typically, however, the behaviors are present even in the absence of substances because over time the chaotic way of communicating has become normal.

Tom and Dana had a Chaos Connection marriage. In order to understand their marriage, you first have to understand a little bit about their backgrounds. Dana's mother was the oldest of nine children. Her father died in World War II while her mother was pregnant with the last child. The mother went to work in a factory and encouraged Dana's mother to drop out of school because she was needed to help out at home. Dana's mother once described herself as "a child raising other children." She quickly found that the only way to maintain order was to be forceful and loud. She settled all issues by making the decision that best suited her at the time, and most quickly quelled whatever disturbance was on the horizon. It worked at the time, and enabled her to run the household in her mother's absence.

Tom's father had grown up the son of an alcoholic building contractor. His father, Tom Sr., had inherited the contracting business from Tom's grandfather who had died in an alcohol-related traffic accident when "Sr." was 23 years old. His grandfather was a "tough old dude," who ruled the family with an iron fist. He controlled the money, the decisions, the business, and the family. When he died, running the family and the business fell to Tom's father to do. And he did it exactly like he had seen his father do it. Tom received very clear and forceful messages about what a "man" was, how to be a "hard workin', hard drinkin' man," and that if you were ever going to "get anywhere in life," it would be because you fought for it. The family message regarding life in general was, "Nothing is going to come easy. You're going to have to learn how to fight for it, and take what you've got coming to you."

Both Tom and Dana had grown up learning that the ordinary way of resolving issues and conflict (from a homeostatic point of view) was to get loud and forceful, and fight for what you wanted. They believed that if you didn't fight for what you wanted, you were going to get left in the dust and not have your needs addressed or met. The concept of *mutuality* had absolutely no place in their backgrounds or their marriage. When we refer to *mutuality* we are defining a process by which the couple agrees, "It (whatever the issue is at the time) must be resolved to the satisfaction of *both of us* as individuals in order to work for the couple." This does not mean that both individuals always get their way, but that there is ultimate agreement on how something is going to be handled.

This was clearly demonstrated one afternoon as Tom and Dana were in a therapy session. They had asked to talk about some problems they were having with their four children. "Why is it that we can't get our children to stop fighting, yelling, throwing things, hitting each other, and going around the house slamming doors?" That was the question they brought to me. Before the end of the session they had yelled at each other, fought over seemingly insignificant issues, yelled at each other, Dana had thrown a pillow at Tom, and Tom had stomped out and slammed the door. Go figure...

Several years ago there was a fascinating movie by the name of "War Games." It starred a young actor named Matthew Broderick who played the part of a computer whiz-kid who accidentally hacked his way into the National Defense Computer System. Finding what he thought was a computer game called "Thermonuclear Warfare," he attempted to download it and, instead, accidentally set up the National Defense computer to initiate a nuclear attack against the then-Soviet Union. As improbable as the scenario was, the movie was most fascinating when the experts couldn't find a way to shut the computer down. Enter our hero. Broderick got the idea of teaching the computer to play Tic Tac Toe against itself. What we see next is every possible combination of Tic Tac Toe being played out on the huge computer screen, each one ending in a draw. After every possible combination had been exhausted, the screen flashed brightly and then went blank. After several seconds, two sentences appeared on the screen. They are what I consider to be one of the best psychological principles for healing the Chaos Connection marriage. The screen read:

"Interesting game The only way to win is *not* to play"

The marriage of the Chaos Connectors cannot exist unless *both* parties consent to "play." If one of the members withdraws, or continues to speak rationally and calmly, addressing the issues instead of attacking the other, the complexion of the marriage changes dramatically. Unfortunately, the individuals involved in these types of relationships have hair-trigger emotions, and once they get *started* it is very difficult to stop, because they have never learned to control their outbursts of negative emotions. Instead, they were taught to use those emotions as a tool or weapon to help them achieve their purpose—to get their way. Making progress with a Chaos Connection is very slow and occurs in very small increments. The process of healing has several levels. First, they must accept the fact that there is another, healthier way to handle issues. Secondly, they must come to terms with the fact that what they were taught in their families of origin was unhealthy and inappropriate. Thirdly, they must be willing to upset the homeostasis of their marriages and commit a conscious act of disloyalty toward their families of origin that initially will feel very uncomfortable. For example, Tom and Dana were making very good strides, one situation at a time, toward resolving conflict in healthy ways, when they went to Tom's house for a Thanksgiving weekend and the whole family was there. They were thrown back into a chaotic situation, and they decided "not to play." They withdrew temporarily, and their withdrawal triggered anxiety and frustration for the rest of the family who couldn't understand why they wouldn't stay and fight it out like they always had. For Tom and Dana, success was measured one situation at a time. Every time the couple resolved a conflict or issue using the new, healthier methods, they rewarded themselves with something—like a movie, or going out to dinner. They both realized something very important about success.

It's not about perfection—it's about direction.

If they could stay on track even most of the time, they could be healthy.

The Lean Machine

There is another form of relationship that we should discuss at this point. It, too, is dramatically impacted by the multigenerational messages passed down from one family to the other—from grandparents, to parents, to children, to grandchildren, and great-grandchildren. I call it the *Lean Machine.* In this case, lean does not mean muscular, or the absence of fat, it means *dependent.* In this particular marriage, both individuals are dependent on the other (leaning on each other) to maintain a certain role or set of behaviors in order for the homeostasis of the marriage to exist. They must lean on each other to exist, and if one of them moves, the other falls down. The relationship typically consists of a *caretaker* and someone who needs to be *taken care of*. We addressed this type of relationship briefly in Chapter One when I referred to "The Case of the Restocked Liquor Cabinet." The relationship can go on indefinitely, and is not as destructive as some of the other types of relationships, like the Chaos Connection, as long as neither individual decides to be *healthier* or more *independent* than they presently are. The unspoken marriage contract consists of two parts: "I'll take care of *you*—and *you* will always be in a position to be taken care of," and, "I'll always be dependent on *you*—and *you* will always take care of me."

Jim and Deb made an appointment to be seen for marital counseling. It was Deb's idea, but Jim did not resist at all. The complaints?

"He is such a slob…and such a baby. I have to take care of him all the time. I'm forever picking up after him. And, I have to make all of his appointments for him. If I didn't call the dentist, his teeth would all fall out. And I don't think this man ever picked up a piece of clothing in his entire life. What does he think I am? His mother? Well, I'm not! God help our children if I ever die. I don't think he knows how to cook anything beside hot dogs, and mac and cheese. Those poor kids. I think I'd will them to my sister. Why, last week he put our three-year-old daughter's blouse on backwards! Can you imagine? He said it looked the same both ways!"

And . . .

"If I had wanted a mother, I would have stayed at home. I had a perfectly good one there. She's forever nagging on me and telling me what I should do every second of the day. I can make my own darn appointments at the dentist. But, *no*, she said that six months from my last appointment was last Thursday, and that I *had* to have an appointment last Thursday. Like, my teeth were going to fall out if I hadn't an appointment next Thursday? I don't think so! And, furthermore, you're right that I don't cook. Not anymore! Every time I ever attempted to cook, she was always looking over my shoulder, telling me what I was doing wrong. Just because I didn't do it *her* way, it was wrong? And lastly, the blouse *did* look the same both ways. How was I to know the buttons went on the back? Who makes shirts with buttons on the back?"

Let's look a little more closely at Jim and Deb from the standpoint of where they come from in their families of origin. Jim was an only child born late in life to a couple who desperately wanted children, but had never been able to conceive. His father was 45 and his mother was 43. It had been a difficult pregnancy and Jim was their "answer to prayer." His father was an attorney with a major airline, and his mother had been a stewardess until age 35. At that time she "retired" and spent her time socializing, gardening, volunteering at a local hospice, and playing tennis. Once Jim was born, all of that changed. She became *mom*. Jim became the center of her life and everything she did revolved around him. So much so that she and her husband were in counseling for a short time because Jim's father felt he was being ignored. Jim's wish was her command. The couple would have huge arguments when Jim's father would try to introduce discipline or suggest work for Jim to do around the house. Nothing extravagant, just what one might expect to instill a sense of personal responsibility in a youth. Jim remembers never having to do chores, never having to make a bed, never having to pick up after himself. "Until I got married," he would add with a scowl. His entire life had been shaped by his mother for one reason only— so she could have someone to take care of. Later on, Jim recalled a statement that his mother made to him while he was engaged to Deb. "You know, you'll never be able to find a woman who is going to take care of you as well as I have." Although he didn't realize it at the time, he came to understand that his mother's form of caretaking deprived him of becoming a responsible adult. What's more, another aspect of his loyalty was to see his wife as *inadequate*. After all, *no one* can be more adequate than mom.

Deb, on the other hand, was the oldest of four siblings, with three brothers who were 6, 9, and 12 years younger than she. She came from a dual-career family with a father who was a swing-shift supervisor at an auto plant, and a mother who worked second shift in a plastics factory. Her role around the house was to be surrogate mother. She was the one constant in her brothers' lives. With mom typically gone when they came home from school, and dad changing shifts every 10 days, she took it upon herself to make sure the boys were cared for. She was affectionately called "Little Mother," and was rewarded for her conscientiousness and ability to maintain order when her parents were not around. When she was old enough to drive, it was Deb who took her brothers to and from school, and to their band concerts and athletic events. Once, she even got into trouble for signing their report cards when they came home with some less than desirable grades. "I guess I was created to be a mother," she would say. "It's all I've ever known, and it's all I've ever been made to feel good about. No one ever told me I was special, or pretty, or smart, or talented. They just told me that I was good at taking care of kids, and that I'd be a great mother some day."

This revelation also helped Deb understand why she had not completed college but had dropped out after one year, at the same time she began dating Jim. She had *found* someone to take care of and that's all that mattered. And Jim had found someone to take care of him. It was the perfect match.

Now that they had children of their own, Deb's needs for "mothering" were being met, and what she was looking for from Jim was more of a mate, a friend, a lover, and a partner. Jim's needs were not being met by any other source, so he was resistant, even though he could state verbally that he didn't want to be taken care of anymore. But it was all he knew. In fact, at one point in the treatment, Jim stated, "I shouldn't have to change. This is just the way I am. Why can't she accept this as one of my character flaws, like a disability." My response was:

> **If you focus on your *disability***
> **rather than on your *capability,***
> **you become a *liability* to the relationship—**
> **and the relationship cannot work!**

In this case, there were two important factors which they both needed to recognize:

1. Jim had never learned how to become an independent adult.
2. Deb had never had the opportunity to really be a child.

Both were required to re-educate themselves to a different way of being that would make them *independent individually* and *interdependent* as a couple, that is, being able to depend on each other, but not being dependent on each other.

The Arrangement

Finally, there is one other relationship that is dramatically impacted by family-of-origin issues. This one is called *the Arrangement*. In this marriage, the relationship has nothing to do with love, or passion, or suitability to the individuals involved. This relationship occurs as a result of the "fit" the individuals have that will meet some specific need in the family of origin. There is nothing new about arranged marriages. They have occurred from the beginning of time. They happened as rewards for some accomplishment, when a king might award the hand of his daughter to a knight who had performed well. Or a marriage might occur to solidify two kingdoms as one, doubling their power base—the daughter of one kingdom's leader marrying the son of another kingdom's leader. History is full of stories recounting the turmoil that these relationships created, especially if the parties involved loved someone else! It's a good thing that this type of marriage is not the rule any longer!

Or perhaps it is...

As we have previously noted (several times, in fact), we are impacted in *every* way by the messages we receive from our families of origin, including specific messages regarding mate selection. If you look back at the BIAS-R you may even be able to pick out some of the criteria set up for you with regard to the kind of mate you might choose. Some of the more prevalent ones include: *Money, religion, level of (and definition of) success, intelligence/wisdom, and politics.*

Daniel and Therese met when he was in eighth grade and she was in seventh. It was an awkward time in their lives, when they fumbled with words and concepts like feelings, and almost everything came out as either arrogance or embarrassment. He was on the eighth-grade football team, and she was on the junior high cheerleading squad as an alternate. Neither one was very accomplished, and they had plenty of time to get to know each other while he was sitting on the bench and she wasn't cheering. They didn't seem to have all that much in common, at first glance. He was from a strict, fundamental Christian home of dual-career, white-collar workers, and she was from a Polish Catholic home of blue-collar workers. But they were friends and that was what kept this adolescent relationship going. She could talk to him about her family and problems she was having at home and he could talk to her about his struggles with grades and conflicts with his parents.

And the relationship grew...

Neither one had very many social skills when it came to dating, so going out with anyone else probably never entered their minds. They were comfortable with one another and as time went on they met each other's families. A bit of a culture shock at first, they both adapted well and began to include the other in family outings. By now, Daniel is in eleventh grade and Therese in tenth, both studying physics and participating in the Physics Club together. Both families seem to have accepted the relationship and are including the two in family weekends away and family picnics. They are now considered a couple. The friendship has developed into what both of them would call love at this point, as much as either of them could identify what that meant. Both had good role models for loving behaviors in their families of origin and had that information to draw on in their own developing relationship. It was a platonic relationship, and both sets of parents did a good job of setting up boundaries (as much as any parents can) that would keep the relationship on a non-sexual level. Daniel went away to college during Therese's senior year of high school. It was during that time that Therese had to decide where to go to college. She wanted to be as close to Daniel as possible if she couldn't go to the same school and much of her decision was based on this.

One evening, around Thanksgiving, Therese came home late from studying at the library to find her parents waiting to talk to her. "This is very difficult for us," they began, "but we've been talking about this a long time and we've come to a decision. We like Daniel very much, but if you decide to marry him, we will have to excommunicate you from the family. He's not Catholic, and those kinds of marriages just don't work. We know this hurts you, but we hope you'll understand some day."

And that was it...

Therese tried to reason with her parents over this issue, but the subject was closed. They had established their position and there was nothing else to talk about.

Therese agonized over what to do. She talked with friends and other family members, but they could not help her. When Daniel came home for Thanksgiving, she broke off the relationship with him. Never telling him the real reason, she told him that she had found someone else and wouldn't see him anymore.

They cried... and went their separate ways.

Daniel's parents told him that it was just as well, because those "mixed marriages don't work out long term anyway." Therese ended up going to a Catholic college on the West Coast, meeting a "nice Catholic boy" who was acceptable to her family, and getting married. Daniel met a "nice Christian girl" who fit all of the criteria for success in his family of origin, and they got married. Although both had married the *right* individual for the family of origin, both were divorced in the first 15 years of marriage. They both remarried, and it was during their second marriages that their paths crossed again, and they spoke of having a relationship—but their marriages were in the way. They sought counseling to help them figure out what to do and decided that they would always carry love one for the other, but that their commitments were toward their current marriages. A healthy decision, although a painful one. For the rest of their lives they will both have a nagging question floating around in the back of their minds—

"I wonder what would have happened if..."

Modern-day arranged marriages are usually far more subtle than the example above. Messages can come in the form of sarcastic, off-handed comments, or a cool reception toward a suitor. The message can come in the form of a passive-aggressive gesture like acting friendly toward the individual when they are present, and putting them down and degrading them when they are not present. Or making jokes about them when they aren't around.

Whatever the devices, they have one intent only—to sway opinion toward the selection of a mate who "fits" properly into the family-of-origin's definition of "acceptable," and help maintain the family homeostasis. Had Therese and Daniel been able to figure out the dynamics of what was occurring in their families, they would have had an opportunity to react differently, perhaps engaging in an act of disloyalty to the family system, or, having given in to the messages, made different decisions about who they *did* marry, in order to be able to sustain that relationship in a healthy way.

We can see clearly how marriages are impacted at every point by the messages we received in our families of origin. In the next chapter we will examine what happens when children arrive on the scene. Do we perpetuate the family system in the next generation? Absolutely! Let's take a look at how that happens. .

Shadowchaser

CONSIDER THE MESSAGES YOU RECEIVED AS REVEALED BY THE BIAS-R. THEN REFLECT ON THE FOLLOWING QUESTIONS:

WHICH MESSAGES DIRECTLY IMPACTED YOUR SELECTION OF A LIFE PARTNER?

WHAT TRAITS DOES YOUR MATE BRING TO THE MARRIAGE THAT ARE SIMILAR TRAITS TO THOSE EXHIBITED BY YOUR OPPOSITE SEX PARENT?

WHAT TRAITS DOES YOUR MATE BRING TO THE MARRIAGE THAT ARE SIMILAR TRAITS TO THOSE EXHIBITED BY YOUR SAME-SEX PARENT?

WHAT TRAITS DO YOU BRING TO THE RELATIONSHIP THAT ARE SIMILAR TO THOSE EXHIBITED BY EITHER OF YOUR MATE'S PARENTS?

WHICH OF YOUR TRAITS CREATE THE MOST BALANCE IN THE RELATIONSHIP?

THE MOST DYSFUNCTION?

WHICH OF YOUR MATE'S TRAITS DO YOU THINK CREATE THE MOST BALANCE IN THE RELATIONSHIP?

THE MOST DYSFUNCTION?

WHAT ISSUES SEEM TO COME UP OVER AND OVER AGAIN IN THE RELATIONSHIP WITHOUT LASTING RESOLUTION?

ARE THOSE ISSUES SIMILAR TO ONES THAT CAME UP IN YOUR FAMILIES OF ORIGIN?

CHAPTER 5

And Baby
Makes Three

"Fathers, don't exasperate your children
by coming down hard on them.
Take them by the hand and lead them
in the way of the Master."
–Ephesians 6:4 The Message

"The first idea that the child must acquire, in order to be actively disciplined,
is that of the difference between good and evil:
and the task of the educator (and parent) lies in seeing
that the child does not confound good with immobility,
and evil with activity...
our aim is to discipline for activity, for work, for good;
not for immobility, not for passivity, not for obedience."
–Maria Montessori

I am a very detail-oriented person... sometimes to my detriment. I was always a multi-focused child—one of those kids who would do homework while talking on the phone, listening to the Beach Boys, and watching Gilligan's Island. Even as an adult, I have a tendency to be extremely aware of things going on around me. Hyper-vigilant might be a clinical term for it. Leaving a restaurant with friends, it is not unusual for me to have also been aware of the conversations at two or three of the surrounding tables. Colette thinks it's rude...but to me it is just part of that focus thing I do. As a result of this ability (disability?), I also have this *other* innate ability to impose that expectation on everyone around me, expecting their focus to also have a very wide beam.

On one occasion, my five-year-old daughter, Chloë, and I were traveling down the freeway, and she pointed *to* the window and asked, "Daddy, what's that?" Looking *through* the window I saw a radio tower with microwave antennas protruding from its top.

"Chloë, that's a radio tower. The radio station plays music, and the sounds of the music are carried on 'waves.' Those waves go from tower to tower until they come down to the antenna in our car. Then it comes out of our radio in the form of music. Those towers also carry the waves for television and daddy's car phone. Isn't that interesting?"

Chloë looked up with disinterest and commented, *"Oh, I thought it was bird poop."*

Ahhh, the lessons we learn from our children. I thought she was pointing *through* the window, and she was pointing *to* the window. She had a much narrower focus than I did at that particular point in time, and she was absolutely right...it *was* bird poop.

One of the easiest elements of dysfunctional behavior which we as parents engage in is the *imposition of our own processes* (the ways we do things or think about things) on our children. If we are intense, we expect that our children will be intense, even if we would prefer they sometimes weren't. If we are laid back and nonchalant about life, there is often a conscious or unconscious imposition of that trait to our children. If I am multi-focused and have a broad beam of awareness, then Chloë should absolutely have those same traits. Why? For the child not to be that way would require a tremendous amount of energy on the part of the parent in terms of controlling and dealing with those behaviors. We have to do far more explaining, defending, rationalizing, disciplining, and creating of boundaries in order to effectively deal with that child. We have to spend far more time involved in answering that question of all questions: *"But why...?"*

"Daddy, why can't we go to Taco Bell for breakfast? I really want a taco. Can we go to Taco Bell for breakfast?"

This was the question of the day for Chloë early last week.

"No, Chloë, tacos are not a breakfast food. We have tacos for lunch and dinner."

"But, why?"

It didn't get any better. Her brother, 8-year-old Nicholas, had been studying Aztec, Mayan, and Mexican archaeology in a summer program at a local university, and had made corn tortillas in his class as part of a project.

"Nicky said in Mexico they have corn tortillas for every meal. Do Mexicans eat breakfast?"

"Yes, Chloë, they do eat breakfast."

"Then, if it's okay for them to have tacos for breakfast, why can't we?"

"Because we're not Mexicans and we're not in Mexico. Besides, Taco Bell isn't even open for breakfast."

"Is Taco Bell open for breakfast in Mexico?"

"*Chloë, that's enough!* We are not having tacos for breakfast because I said so! Now, be quiet and eat your bagel!"

"Daddy, do they have bagels in Mexico?"

"*Chloë...!*"

I look at her sternly and her tears begin to flow.

"You just don't understand me..."

On the one hand, it would be so much easier if she simply accepted everything I said without question. No fuss, no muss. But, she would not be a healthy child for doing so. Albert Einstein once observed, "The important thing is *not to stop questioning.*" As parents it is imperative that we understand that *easier* is *not* always *better,* and that a questioning child is not a bad child, or out of line for having asked the questions. We must teach our children healthy and appropriate processes with which they *can* question, and therefore learn what they need to know in order to get along in their worlds, that is, the world as they *experience* it. This includes how we define our world differently than our children, both specifically and conceptually.

We must realize that the focus of every child, and the way they define their world is going to be very different than we do or would, and if we can accept that fact, and begin to meet them *where they are,* rather than *where we want or expect them to be because of where **we** are,* we have the best opportunity to raise healthy children.

Shadowchaser

THINK FOR A MOMENT ABOUT YOUR OWN CHILDREN. CONSIDER THE FOLLOWING QUESTIONS.

WHAT PRIMARY TRAIT DO YOU SEE IN THEM THAT IS A REFLECTION OF YOUR OWN PERSONALITY?

WHAT TRAIT DO YOU SEE IN THEM THAT IS A REFLECTION OF YOUR MATE'S PERSONALITY?

WHAT ABOUT THOSE SIMILARITIES AMUSES YOU?

IS THERE ANYTHING ABOUT THOSE SIMILARITIES THAT DISTURBS YOU?

If certain issues carry important meaning to us, then we have a desire and expectation, spoken or not, that our children will carry with them the same meaning, and the same intensity toward that issue as we do. This is done *even if the personality of the child is genetically different than that of the parent.* There is significant research that demonstrates that personality is developed from the genetic base as well as the familial, social, and cultural. There is a verse of Bible scripture which says, "Train a child in the way he should go, and when he is old he will not turn from it." (Proverbs 22:6 NIV) The Hebrew translation of that particular verse offers an interesting insight into child rearing. It says, "Train your children in the *way which they are bent,* and when they are old, they will not depart from it." That places an entirely different slant on the concept. If we are able to raise our children according to their own unique gifts and personalities, rather than to functionally mold them into what *we "need" them to be,* we can then teach them to use that personality to their *benefit* rather than to *our benefit,* and their *deficit.* If the child does not carry out our impositions, it takes us, as parents, out of our comfort zones to have to deal with the differences, and we will try to bring the child into alignment with our needs and expectations in an effort to stay in our comfort zones.

As we have mentioned previously, these impositions are very often multigenerational, passed down from family to family. They are also functional, at least at some point and to some generation. They were instituted to provide an extremely important *function* to the family, and out of family *loyalty,* the behaviors are maintained and sustained consistently, specifically, and behaviorally. Whichever the case, they are imposed for one reason and one reason only—to *maintain the homeostasis* in the family system.

In my paternal grandfather's generation, working was more important than education, and all of the men in the family, during that generation, were very hard-driving and industrious blue-collar workers. My grandfather took his work very seriously, and I don't recall ever hearing that he missed a day of work, although I'm sure he did. His expectation for himself was that he would work at the same place until retirement, and then fish. And he did. Earning a living to support the family, and doing whatever it took to earn that living, was the top priority for him. Throw in a war and the Great Depression, and "doing whatever it took" began to take on a different meaning—it meant survival. One of the multigenerational messages I received about family growing up as a Beighley was:

"You will do whatever it takes to support your family, even if it means having more than one job or digging ditches, like your grandfather did."

There was no negative connotation to hard physical labor, but for that generation it was the labor, not the education, that was important.

For my father's generation, providing for the family was just as important. The same message applied to all of the men in his family of that generation. Providing for the family was the most critical responsibility. But, in this generation, education began to take on a slightly different meaning. The message began to change to,

*"You will do whatever it takes to support your family, even if it means having more than one job, or digging ditches like your grandfather, but education will help you get ahead, and perhaps not have to work **so hard** to support that family."*

My father heard that message and, while working full time to support the family, he began to get additional training and take classes that would help him advance in his job. He saw the benefits of education, and how that could help him work smarter, not harder.

Then I came along. The only male child in the nuclear family. And the message I heard took on even a more explicit educational slant, but still retained the emphasis on supporting the family. The message became:

*"You will do whatever it takes to support your family. You **will** get a college education and go as far as you can with it to get the best possible job doing what **you** want to do, and making a good living at it."*

There was no doubt in my mind that I would earn a Ph.D. From the fourth grade my dream for the future began with these words: "When I get my doctorate…" It was not clear, of course, *what* I might get that doctorate in, and that changed several times before the process was finished. Only the education mattered.

At 22, my oldest son, Nathan, is one of ten crew members on a large yacht owned by the Amway Corporation. He sails all over the world. It's hard work, but he loves it and gets paid well. It was never how I pictured him at 22. After all, the messages I had sent him over his lifetime were very clear and, I thought, "binding." This, you see, is a great danger for parents:

*That we are not only aware of the messages we send, but that we consider them to be **binding** to our children when, in fact, they may not be in the best interest of the child.*

When he was in high school, we began to investigate possible colleges for him to attend. It was never an issue of "whether or not," it was only a matter of "which." Of course, Dad wanted him to go to one of my alma maters, but ultimately he chose a small, private Christian college in Indiana. The messages he had received regarding education and supporting a family were very clear, but an additional generational slant was created as I sent the message to him over the years. It looked like this:

"You will do whatever it takes, to get a good college education and take that as far as you can in order to position yourself to take the best care of and support your family."

After he completed his first year, he came home and told us, "Mom and Dad, I don't have a clue. I don't have any idea about what I want to do or how I want to do it. Until that happens and until I get some other focus, college is a waste of time and money. I'm not going to go back next year. Maybe in a few years. I don't know. I just need to do some other things right now."

My heart sank to the floor and my stomach ended up in my throat.

And although I hated to admit it, my initial thoughts were, "How could he do this to me. He *knows* how important it is to me that he get a good college education. Doesn't he know how this will affect me?"

You may have noticed how many times I used the word *"me"* in those sentences. What Nathan did was commit an act of *disloyalty* to the Beighley Family System, an act of treason toward a message that had been handed down, and honed, and perfected over at least three generations. It was not a deliberate act to make me crazy. It was not an intentional in-your-face type of behavior. In fact, it was not other-destructive or self-destructive at all, but an honest assessment of where he was at the time, and what he needed in order to be "Nathan." He had taken all of the processes and information we had given him for 19 years and used them to come to a good decision for himself. He had done it *just as we had taught him.* Imagine that... Now, if only *I* could let go of my expectations for him, and let him do what I taught him to do...everything would be okay!

And I did.

And it was.

We recently received a phone call from Nathan. He was with the yacht off one of the Greek Islands. He shared what had been going on with himself, the rest of the crew, and some of the sights he had seen and things he had done. He thanked us for the birthday present we had sent, and then, somewhat hesitantly, asked our opinion *one more time* about how we felt regarding his being on the boat.

My heart sank again!

I was somehow certain, initially, that we *still* hadn't gotten across to Nathan that if this was his chosen direction at this time in his life, and he was contented with that decision, then we were very happy for him— because his joy in life was the most important thing. When I checked out with him my concern, he responded,

"That's what I *thought* you would say. *I just needed to hear it again.*"

Another lesson from my children! It is not only important that we affirm them for their healthy decisions. It is just as important that we *reaffirm* them on an ongoing basis, and realize that it is *our job* as parents to actively pursue opportunities to affirm them for what they do.

Now, the other side of the coin demanded a bit of self-analysis, which is good in moderation and can lead to personal growth, but which is paralyzing and destructive if taken to an extreme. I had to examine whether or not I had inadvertently sent him a message in which his response of leaving college would have been an act of loyalty, not disloyalty. Did I send him a "no competition" message, or a message that indicated I would not have been able to handle it if he were "more successful" than I. I believe the answer was "no," but that Nathan had chosen to *define his criteria for success* differently for himself at this time in his life. As we look at both sides of the coin our awareness will usually help us sort out the function of the new behaviors we defined, at first glance, as dysfunctional, but do, however, have a positive functional meaning in our lives.

Most of the impositions we place on our children are intended to create and enforce *likeness,* an adherence to what we desire to be true, what we need to be true, or what we need to happen. I was once called upon to do an evaluation on two sisters, ages four and six. And even at those tender ages they already were known in their area as chronic shoplifters. When these girls went into a store it was a given that they would try to leave the store with something they had not purchased. This happened whether or not they were with their single-parent mother. From the standpoint of normal childhood development, it would have been far more understandable if they had been stealing candy, gum, small toys, or clothes for their Barbie dolls. They weren't. They were stealing food and household supplies. They were shoplifting canned corn, meat, toilet paper, soap—the essentials for daily living. And, each time they were caught, their reaction was not anger or shame. It was *confusion.* Ultimately, the evaluation revealed that the girls were confused about being reprimanded and punished (and finally taken away from their mother) for something they had been taught all of their lives was good and expected, something for which they would be rewarded when successful.

The mother, who had no history of personal shoplifting, and no criminal record, had imposed upon her daughters the dysfunctional behavior of stealing to meet her own personal needs. She argued that the needs were not frivolous—they were survival needs. And in evaluating *her* background we found very clear messages disregarding principles of right and wrong. The principles she had been raised with were:

"You do whatever it takes to get what you need— if you need it, **take** *it."*

Her father had regularly come home with materials he would take from the shop where he worked, saying, "They'll never miss it anyway, and besides, I needed it." In this family the messages condoning and even promoting the dysfunctional behaviors had been passed down through at least three generations, with each one becoming a little more dulled of conscience, and the lines between right and wrong becoming just a little more blurry. When finally it reached these two young girls, the lines were not only blurry, they were invisible. They were convinced what they were doing was right. They were unable to distinguish it from wrong.

In psychology there is a defense mechanism called "projective identification" in which an individual *projects* a part of themselves that they deem unacceptable upon someone else and attributes the characteristic to that other person as a way to explain the dysfunction. For example, if I have a need to see myself as a really nice guy who is very tolerant and gets along with everyone, and I have a conflict with you that impairs the relationship and my image of myself, I can split off that part of me and give it to you. It now becomes, "You don't like me and don't want to resolve issues with me—that's why the relationship can't work." This is most often not a conscious act, but a defense which allows us to maintain a perception of ourselves even when it isn't true. Unfortunately, one of the primary sources on which to project these attributes is often our children. This imposition on our children is based not on likeness, but on *differences.* And one of the messages sent to the child is, "I need you to do this (or "be" this, or "perform in this way") because I can't ("don't want to" or "can't bring myself to") and you can because we're different."

Jennifer hated men. She didn't merely dislike them, or have no use for them, or just have a difficult time when she was around them. Jennifer *hated* men!

She was 24, had never been married, and had gone through a long series of short relationships. "Guys consider themselves to have had a successful relationship with me if, when they call me after the first date, I don't

tell them where to go. Of course, very few call me after the first date."
She could laugh about it on the surface, but Jennifer felt alone and isolated, and longed for a loving relationship and someone to share with. "I don't understand it," she would tell me. "I really want to get to know guys, to let them get to know me, but it seems everything they do *irritates* me! No offense to you." This was a long-standing feeling. In fact, Jennifer could not remember a time when she *didn't* feel this way. She was an only child of parents who had divorced when she was two. She had not seen her father since the divorce, although he had attempted to contact her several times over the past two years and she had refused to see him. "He's just another jerk," she would tell me. "He abandoned me and mom, even though she tried for years to get him back. She did everything…and nothing worked. He treated her like garbage after they were divorced, and she *still* wanted to get him back. She was really sweet, and did a lot of things for him. What a jerk! Although she was pretty stupid, too, for hanging in there so long."

Jennifer's mother had never remarried.

Realizing that she was two when the divorce took place, I asked her how she had remembered so much of what happened at such an early point in her life. After considering the question she replied, "I'm not sure how much I really *do* remember myself. I just remember mom talking about it and crying, and being all upset all the time." She continued by relating that mom's despair really took hold when Jennifer was in her teens and had begun to develop relationships with boys. She recalls one instance clearly when her mother's statements really confused her.

Jennifer had come home from school and mentioned that a boy in her Spanish class had asked her to go to the football game and dance afterward on Saturday night. She had declined because, she told her mother, "the guy can be a bit of a snob sometimes." Her mother's reply caught her by surprise. "Jennifer, it's not good that you hate boys so much. They aren't *all* like your father. And not all of them are perfect, either. If you keep being so choosy and showing how much you dislike them, you'll never have a relationship."

"I remember thinking," Jennifer said, "that I didn't even know I had a problem with boys. In fact, I didn't think I did, and don't recall ever saying any other negative thing to my mom about boys. But if she said I had a problem with boys, I guess I must have had a problem with boys! After all, she was the mother."

This was the beginning of Jennifer's "hatred" toward men, and her mother's unconscious advocacy of that emotion. Throughout Jennifer's adolescence her mother would tell her that her hate and disdain of men was not healthy, how she would never be in a relationship with that attitude, that she would never marry because no man would put up with her.

And Jennifer began to behave consistently with what she was learning about herself!

Early in the therapy Jennifer invited her mother to attend. The goal: to hear from her mother what the mother's experience of her own divorce and subsequent relationship with her ex-husband was like for her. "I never really understood *why* he divorced me," she said, "and that's what made it so hard. One day he was there—and the next he said he didn't love me any more and wanted to be out of the relationship."

"How did you feel when he left," Jennifer asked.

"I was afraid, and lonely, and wanted him back."

"Weren't you angry?"

"No, I would have done anything to get him back. If I had been angry with him, I never would have had a chance."

"Mother, just because you didn't act angry doesn't mean you weren't angry. What did you do with your anger? You must have had some after all the things you told me he did to you."

"I don't know. I really don't know what I did with my anger. Maybe I didn't think I needed to be angry. After all *you were angry enough for both of us.*"

Jennifer's mother was exactly right. Jennifer had been carrying her mother's anger for all of those years, in addition to her own for having been abandoned by her father. And the mother *needed* to *not* be angry, even if she was. She couldn't afford to be angry if she was going to have an opportunity to salvage her marriage, so she had to split the angry part of her off, and give it to a "loyal" daughter who was unconsciously willing to carry it for her. As Jennifer could begin to understand that she had been carrying her mother's *projected anger,* she began to learn how to sort out what was hers, and what was her mother's and *not hold on* to emotions that were not hers. She also began to be able to establish relationships with men based on each individual, rather than giving them a global assessment. "I think all men *might be* jerks," she would laugh. "But, at least I'm willing to give them a chance to show me something different."

There are two other related methods by which we impose on our children the messages and roles which are necessary to maintain homeostasis and family loyalty within the system. They are *scripting* and the *self-fulfilling prophecy. Scripting* is a mechanism by which we "write out" the roles we want the child to play, and we teach the child the "script" for that role, much the same way an actor might prepare for a film role. The actor would study the script, and try in every way to *become* that person, so that the movie might seem more real. In family systems, the scripting of the role becomes who that child is very often, and when the child has fully adopted the role prescribed for them, they have *fulfilled the prophecy,* and completed the function for the family.

Father Andrew was a priest. And he loved being a priest. He could not remember a time when he hadn't wanted to be a priest. "In fact," he would say, "I was a priest long before I ever became a priest." Born James Andrew O'Shannon, he was the child who was never supposed to be. His parents had attempted conceiving many times, all without success. His mother had tried hormones, *in vitro* fertilization, having the linings of her uterus treated to make conception easier, all without success. She had had four miscarriages and the doctors had advised her not to have any more pregnancies. She was being told to "give up" because there was a fear that her body could suffer damage and she could put herself at risk if she continued on her quest to have children naturally. She and her husband were heartbroken. A devout Catholic family, they attended Mass regularly and were heavily involved in the work of the parish. They had prayed that God would intervene on their behalf and send them a child. "After all," his mother said, "it worked for Abraham and Sarah. Why couldn't it work for me?"

Father Andrew's own father had given up hope completely. He had focused his attention on other things, and only thought about having a child when the subject was raised by his wife.

But, she never gave up, and continued to pray.

Then, at age 46, she became pregnant again. She was shocked by the development, but continued to pray. "Lord, if you give me this child, a healthy child, I promise to give that child back to you to do Your work. Just give me a healthy child." The pregnancy was a difficult one, but nine months later, James Andrew O'Shannon was born. And his parents dedicated him back to God, just as they said they would.

"Jimmy" went to catechism, attended an all-boys Catholic grade school, and a Catholic high school. He was an altar boy, sang in the choir, and helped the priests during the week. He was well known around the rectory as a polite, studious, and helpful boy. And all along the way he continued to hear the same message from his parents:

"You're going to make a fine priest someday."

It was not "maybe," or "if God calls you." It was a pure and simple message, consistently, from the beginning all through his life: He was going to be a priest. He accepted the role, fulfilled the script, and in the end became a priest, just as he had been told. In becoming that priest, he had fulfilled a commitment by his parents to "return him to God," and thus fulfilled the prophecy set forth for him.

He was able to later reflect: "It took me some time to figure out whether this was my calling, or the calling of my parents for me. I really believe it *was* my calling, but that the calling was as a result of the commitment my parents made to God before I was even born. It fits for me...who I am, and what my personality is like...it was meant to be."

Greg was an avid reader. He learned to read very early under the tutelage of his mother, a school librarian, and he caught on very well. During the day, his mother often had to take books away and send him outside to play with other friends. "You can't stay in here all the time with your nose stuck in a book. Go outside and get some fresh air." At night, his parents often caught him reading in bed by the glow of his night light, or with a flashlight under his blankets.

Greg really liked to read!

So, it was probably not a surprise to anyone when he began to be scripted as either a "librarian like his mother" or an "English teacher, because he has such a passion for reading." As his skills improved, so did his opportunities to participate in different areas that would send him in the direction of the script. His poetry got published in junior and senior high, he was on the debate team and forensics team, he worked his way through the ranks and became editor of the school newspaper. He went to college as an education major, and not only worked on the college newspaper, but also wrote for the local city newspaper as well. And during this time his passion for reading never ended. He was an insatiable reader whose desk and night stand were always covered with books.

In his senior year of college he was offered a contract to teach at the college level, an unheard-of offer at the time. He could teach and at the same time pursue his graduate degree. The prophesy was being fulfilled! Greg was going to be a "teacher."

Six months into the contract, Greg quit. Everyone was shocked at this turn of events, including Greg. "I hated it," he would later say. "I hated every minute of it, and I couldn't understand why. I would prepare, and teach, and then go home depressed and angry all the time. Then it hit me!

"I never wanted to be a teacher. I only wanted to read.

"And I especially resented teaching something that meant *so much to me* to 300 bonehead freshmen who couldn't care less. So, I figured it was time to do something else. Something where people could come to me because they really wanted to, not because they had to."

Greg went on to graduate school and became a social worker, and created his own criteria for success. It was extremely difficult for him because he met with all types of resistance, especially from his family who had scripted him to begin with. He felt *guilt* for having been disloyal to the family, and *anger* over having been scripted in the first place. After working hard to *push through* these issues, he was able to establish new and healthy *independent* relationships with his family, and fully invest himself in his new calling.

John Madison was in prison. He had been in a bar brawl and had killed another man while drunk. He couldn't afford an attorney, and the public defender didn't have much to work with, since John had been convicted twice before on assault charges. There was also a history of domestic violence, and the police had been at his home several times previously after his wife had called 911. Each instance was connected to alcohol, but John insisted he didn't have a drinking problem and never sought treatment.

John Madison had a son.

John Madison, Jr., was four and a half years old when his father went to prison. His mother moved in with her own mother, since she couldn't support the boy and his two older sisters by herself. "Junior," as he was called, was the spitting image of his father. Dark hair, dark eyes and olive skin, jutting chin, he "sauntered" around the house "just like his father used to." He was all boy and challenged his mother and grandmother on a regular basis. And their response was typically the same.

"Boy, if you're not careful, you're gonna end up in prison, just like your worthless daddy."

In fifth grade he was suspended for smoking in the school restroom.

In sixth grade he was suspended for fighting in class. After the third such suspension, he was expelled and sent to another school district.

In the seventh grade he started drinking and experimenting with marijuana. He was suspended four times that year for fighting and smoking in school.

In the eighth grade he was sent to an alternative classroom because he couldn't "get along" in the regular classroom. He skipped over 80 days of school that year. He would often come home in the middle of the day, intoxicated or stoned.

In the ninth grade he stopped going to school. No amount of threats by the school or his mother and grandmother had any impact on him. He spent his time with friends, hanging out, drinking, and smoking dope. His mother had a suspicion that he had graduated to crack cocaine, but she could never prove it. That year he was charged twice with "breaking and entering," and convicted once. He was to be sentenced in two weeks.

After each suspension, expulsion, episode of drinking or drugs, after each encounter with teachers, principals, law enforcement officials, and the court system, he would hear the same thing.

*"I **told you**, if you don't stop that stuff you are gonna end up just like your daddy. If you live long enough, someday you're gonna end up in prison."*

In September of 1990, John Madison, Jr., would have been 15 years old. His grandmother got the call that his body had been found in an abandoned and boarded-up house five blocks away from their own. An anonymous caller had telephoned the police to tell them. And through their pain, all both his mother and grandmother could say was,

*"We **knew** this was going to happen. He had been heading in this direction all his life."*

It is, I firmly believe, the job of the parents to shape and mold their children. The key, I think, is to be consciously—sometimes painfully—aware of *how* you are shaping them. Is it *self-serving* to meet your needs as a parent, or is it *self-actualizing* for the child, teaching them to understand themselves and use that information to grow into what they need to grow into with your help? We really need to stay on the self-actualizing end of the spectrum, as much as possible, and we can only do that through awareness of the messages we are sending.

And through that same awareness, we can move from the dysfunctional personal behaviors that we engage in and subsequently pass down to our children, to create new and healthy behaviors which will help us live as healthy families.

Shadowchaser

THINK OF A "COOKIE CUTTER," THE KIND YOUR MOTHER USED TO MAKE SUGAR COOKIES IN A VARIETY OF SHAPES. NOW THINK OF THE EMOTIONAL, INTELLECTUAL, AND SPIRITUAL COOKIE CUTTER YOU HAVE CREATED FOR YOUR CHILDREN. WHAT IS THE "SHAPE" YOU BELIEVE YOU HAVE BEEN PROVIDING FOR THEM AS THEY HAVE GROWN OVER THE YEARS? IS IT A POSITIVE SHAPE, OR PERHAPS ONE THAT CARRIES NEGATIVE CONNOTATIONS? DOES IT FIT WITH WHAT YOU HAVE SEEN AS THEIR "BENT", OR DOES IT APPEAR THAT IT BETTER SUITS THE PERSONALITIES OF YOU AND/OR YOUR MATE? WHAT IS *YOUR* GOAL FOR YOUR CHILD?

CHAPTER 6

The Pattern Maker

"When I was an infant at my mother's breast
I gurgled and cooed like any infant.
When I grew up, I left those infant ways for good.
We don't yet see things clearly.
We're squinting in the fog, peering in a mist.
But it won't be long before the weather clears and the sun shines bright!"
–I Corinthians 13:11 The Message

"If one advances confidently in the direction of his dreams,
and endeavors to live the life which he has imagined,
he will meet with a success unexpected in common hours."
–Henry David Thoreau

"I have learned that success is to be measured
not so much by the position that one has reached in life
as by the obstacles which he has overcome while trying to succeed."
–Booker T. Washington

Nathan was eight and Collin, his brother, was four when we were taking a walk along the American River in Northern California. It was January, cool and clear, and the river was fueled by meltdown from the snow pack in the Sierra Nevada mountain range. We had been walking for quite some time, and the exercise helped all of us work up a healthy sweat. We stopped along a beautiful part of the river to take a rest, and Collin asked, "Daddy, can we take off our shoes and socks and walk in the water?"

"No, Collin, it's still winter and that water is *freezing* cold. We'll do it another time when it's warmer."

"Okay," he answered.

We continued our walk, and about ten minutes later Collin asked, "Daddy, can we take off our shoes and socks and walk in the water?"

"Collin, I already answered that question. It's too cold today. You'll catch a death of a cold and your mother will have a fit. We can't go in the water today. Be content that we're taking this walk. It's a really beautiful day."

"Okay," he answered.

We continued our walk, and it wasn't even ten minutes later when Collin asked again,

"Daddy, can we take off our shoes and socks and walk in the water?"

I had had enough!

*"**Collin**...I told you, the water is too cold, you would catch pneumonia, your mother would have a fit, and **It's not going to happen!**"*

Collin thought for a moment, looked up, put his hands on his hips, and said, "If you were a *kid,* you'd let us."

We *all* took off our shoes and socks and walked in the frigid waters of the American River. We had a *great time.* No one got sick, no one caught pneumonia, no one got swept downstream. It was a highly successful outing, and we made a wonderful memory that afternoon.

Was I manipulated by a four-year-old? No, not really. I *was,* however, challenged to think through my reasons for saying no, and, more importantly, to review and evaluate my *specific and behavioral criteria for success* for our little walk in the woods along the river.

What was my goal? What was I trying to accomplish? How would I know if I had accomplished it? All important questions that not only apply to a walk along the river, but in every endeavor that we pursue. All too often we rush into things and situations without taking the appropriate time to consider, "What am I doing here? What is my goal? And, even more importantly, how will I know when I've achieved it? On what am I going to base my *success?*" Let's explore what we are now going to *do* with our newfound awareness and knowledge of our family systems, the roles we played in them, and, in the light of what we now know, our consideration of what we would *choose* to change in our lives.

Having identified our dysfunctional behaviors, we now have a splendid opportunity to create new and healthy *patterns* for our lives.

These *new and healthy patterns* will consist of the following elements:

1. **The *new and healthy patterns* will come about as a result of our *conscious awareness* of how the family system worked,** the role we played in it, and the functions of our unhealthy behaviors in that family system. All of

the ways we worked to maintain the family-system homeostasis come into play here. This can be compared to having a box that contains a puzzle, but has no picture on the front of the box to give you any clue as to what you are building. You begin with one piece, find another that fits into it, and now you have a bigger piece. Slowly, you put more and more pieces together and begin to get a picture of what is happening. As small parts of the picture begin to make themselves clearer, the larger picture also begins to take more shape. And the process continues until you can look at all of the pieces you have available to you and be able to determine what the missing pieces *probably* looked like. And using all of the information available to you, you then look at all you have compiled and say,

> *"Now I understand.*
> *Now I see where I fit.*
> *Now I see how my behavior played an important function.*
> *Now I see what the family was trying to accomplish.*
> *Now I understand... and can choose do something about it."*

2. **The *new and healthy patterns* will be conscious acts of disloyalty to dysfunctional behaviors** we engaged in throughout our lives in our nuclear families. I often tell clients, "Working with me is both a *blessing* and a *curse*. The blessing is that you will learn new ways of functioning and have a chance to establish a healthy lifestyle. The curse is that you are going to have me dancing around in the back of your psyche for the rest of your life, and will never again be able to pretend that you didn't know better. For now, you know too much!"

3. **The *new and healthy patterns* will begin with a decision to engage in new types of healthy behaviors** necessary to accomplish newly established goals for the direction of our lives. It *all* begins with the *decision*. There is an ancient saying attributed to the Chinese, I believe, that says, "A journey of a thousand miles begins with a single step," and what precedes that single step is the decision to take it. Decision-making is a dynamic process, not a static process. There is a dictum of family therapy that says, *"Not to decide is to decide."* This quote is evidence that we can live life by *design* or by *default*. In living life by design, *we* make the decisions and proceed forward, acknowledging that with our decisions come responsibility, capability, and accountability along with the potential for result and reward. We have made choices and there is no place

for blaming others for the direction of our lives.

When we choose to *not* decide, the decision ultimately gets made for us by others as a result of our inactivity, inability, or inattentiveness to the details of what must occur to get us to the next step. We voluntarily give up our right to control what occurs to us, and give that right to someone or some circumstance to take control over us. It is from this position that we most often project blame upon others. I am reminded of a joke that goes,

Question: *"What is an American's favorite wine?" (read "whine")*
Answer: *"It's not my fault..."*

Our increased willingness to make our own healthy decisions and take responsibility for them come with two things: *the equivalent level of accountability and the potential for successful living beyond what we have previously known!*

4. **The *new and healthy patterns* will contain specific and behavioral criteria for success** which, when done consistently, will allow us to establish a new and healthy pattern for our lives. In doing this step we develop *consistency.* And consistency is one of the most important elements of healthy change, because it allows us to become comfortable with the changes over time and be able to trust them. I have an equation for *trust:*

$$\text{TRUST} = \frac{\text{CONSISTENCY}}{\text{TIME}}$$

As we are able to be consistent over time with our new patterns of behavior based on specific and behavioral criteria for success, we have a renewed opportunity to make them the natural part of our personality makeup, not just an occasional exception.

5. **The *new and healthy patterns* will not feel comfortable initially,** even if they are healthy, because they have forced us out of the comfort that our dysfunction provided for us as the known and expected parts of our lives.

A young couple that I had married a few years earlier returned to see me for a "50,000 mile checkup," and the young man was discouraged. When I asked why they had come to see me, he replied, "Dr. Beighley, this is hard."

"Excuse me?"

"This is really hard...this health stuff. I mean, you have to work at it every day."

"Yes...?"

"You don't get it. It is *really hard! I thought it would get easier over time and I wouldn't have to work at it all the time. It's just too hard.*"

I "got it!" I was just waiting for him to tell me something I *didn't* know, or something that was a *problem*. It is not a problem to face the fact that being healthy is hard. It's a fact of life and an opportunity to change. It's an acknowledgment of a line in a John Lennon song—"Life is what happens when you have other plans." Those are the facts— not the problems.

The problems arise when we go into denial about the facts.

The problems occur when we refuse to acknowledge that healthy living is not a cake walk, and that we're going to have to work for it in order to enjoy it. The problems occur when, out of fear, we make a conscious decision *not* to change our unhealthy behaviors because we're afraid of upsetting the homeostasis of an unhealthy system. Those are problems. Healthy living presents us with a wonderful *opportunity* to be who God always intended us to be. And—it is hard...

6. **While engaging in our *new and healthy behaviors*, we will recognize that this endeavor of healthy living is not a goal, but an ongoing process,** which will go through continual evaluation and change throughout our entire lives. A rabbi friend of mine once shared that he felt the greatest sin which mankind in general was guilty of committing was the *sin of complacency*—that is, settling for the status quo in life, as opposed to pursuing life to its fullest, accepting all of the challenges of being a healthy individual, and making the absolute most out of every day.

Let's take a look at what steps are involved in creating our *new and healthy behaviors*, and in determining a new pattern complete with specific and behavioral criteria for success for our lives. We will break this down into several sections which will give you a partial list of important issues for your life plan. You can then expand the list to include those other issues which are of importance to you personally, but were not included on this list. You will recognize most of this list has been borrowed from the BIAS-R. This makes good sense because those were the common issues for which we received our primary life messages in our families of origin. We must now *re-evaluate* them as to their applicability to your specific choices for a healthy lifestyle, and establish the criteria which will allow you to determine whether or not you are headed in the right direction. This will become your initial road map to health. It's not a rigid, unbending set of rules, but, rather, a set of guidelines you can adjust as you *go and grow.*

The Nature of Success

We must first consider what "success" means. It is a dynamic definition, one that changes with individuals and circumstances, and one size does *not* fit all. The question of *success* has triggered many comments from many different sources which lend themselves to the enigma and confusion that this concept often carries with it.

Ben Sweetland is credited with saying, *"Success* is a journey, not a destination."

From Henry David Thoreau we hear, "Why should we be in such desperate haste to succeed, and in such desperate enterprises? If a man does not keep pace with his companions, perhaps it is because he hears a different drummer."

An Emily Dickinson poem reads, *"Success* is counted sweetest/By those who ne'er succeed."

"We live in a war of two antagonistic ethical philosophies, the ethical policy taught in the books and schools, and the *success* policy." –William Graham Spencer

"Success is the one unpardonable sin against one's fellows." —Ambrose Bierce

And, finally, from Cindy Adams, *"Success* has made failures of many men."

These views are as diverse as the individuals who said them and the situations which prompted them. We certainly can see that creating a personal, specific, and behavioral criteria for success will present a worthy challenge to creating a solid foundation for our growth and fulfillment.

Nicholas has been on the community swim team for the first time this summer. He swims in the 8-and-under category and has been working hard with his coach to learn the different strokes. He has had swimming lessons for several years and is very comfortable in the water, so being on the swim team sounded like a good idea to him. There was only one thing that he hadn't counted on—*competition.*

"You mean we have to *beat* other people?"

His coach, Mr. Parks, clarified that notion immediately in what I felt was a very affirming and healthy way, and in his response helped Nicholas to begin to establish a criteria for success for himself as a rookie on the swim team.

"Nicholas," he said, "sometimes you might be able to beat other people, sometimes maybe you won't. The important thing for you to concentrate on is *not* whether you beat other people, but whether or not you improve your *own* times each time you have a meet. That is *your* goal, and it is different from anyone else on the swim team. And I'm going to teach you how to do that."

Nicholas had a swim meet yesterday. It was his final meet of the summer. There were eight other cities competing in the meet, and we knew it was going to last most of the afternoon. Colette and I were there to cheer him on, and Chloë was there as his primary cheerleader, screaming from the balcony, "Go, Bubba, go. Go, Bubba, go."

Nicholas was scheduled to swim in two races, the 25-meter front crawl, and the 25-meter backstroke. He was ranked 21 of 22 in the front crawl, and 14 of 22 in the backstroke, and was really pumped up for this meet. When it came time for his heat in the front crawl he looked like a little Olympian on the starting block. The gun sounded, and he dove in with the rest of the boys. With his coach walking on the side of the pool urging him on, and with the parents all screaming their heads off, Nicholas was moving his arms and legs just as fast as he could...all the way down the pool. It was a wonderful race (aren't they all, for parents) and I think he finished third in his heat. The important thing was this—*he had cut 12 seconds off his best previous time!* We were ecstatic! And so was he. As soon as he got out of the pool, a timer congratulated him and gave him a blue "Best Time" ribbon. He had been successful beyond what he (or any of us, for that matter) had ever expected. *And that's all that counted.*

That same evening, we watched the Olympics from Atlanta, Georgia, on television. The women's 50-meter freestyle was on and Amy VanDyken from the United States was trying to win her fourth gold medal and do something no American woman had ever done—win the 50-meter freestyle in the Olympics. It was a fast and exciting race, with the Chinese swimmer in the lead until the last few seconds. Amy touched less than a second before her opponent, and won the race. What a finish! It was great to watch.

Nicholas' comment? "That was really good…but did she cut 12 seconds off her time?"

It is important to understand that before we begin to define or measure success corporately, we must first define it individually. Any other way of looking at it will be an exercise of futility, because we will not have a personal yardstick and not be able to place ourselves in *situations appropriate to our competencies.*

Let's examine some issues:

Family

What is your criteria for success for your family? First, we have to define what family is. We did this in Chapter One, and for use in this exercise we will define the family as a nuclear one; you, your spouse, your children, and any other extended family member living in the home with you. Having defined that, we'll move on to the important questions that require a specific and behavioral answer.

"What would my healthy family look like to me?"

Think specifically how you believe your family would look if it were functioning in a healthy and appropriate way, considering the situations in which each family member finds himself or herself. Does success mean the following for *your family?* Adjust each of the following statements until it fits what you believe would be healthy in your situation. Below each of the points listed below, write in *your* adaptation of the trait. Be sure that your response is "behavioral," not general. "I want us to get along" is a general statement that leaves too much open to interpretation. "We will speak with one another calmly, without screaming, yelling, raised voices, or physical outbursts" is a specific statement.

We eat at least one meal a day together, at least five days a week.

Response:_____

Sunday evening meal together is a top priority.

Response:_____

There will be no radio, television, stereo, or reading at the table during meal times.

Response:_____

We will eat at the dining room table, at the same time, together.

Response:_____

We will hold hands and pray together before every meal, even when dining out.

Response:_____

We will have family devotions after meals when eating in. We will take turns reading a devotional and praying.

Response:_____

Thursday evening is "date night" for mom and dad. Kids will have a sitter (or fend for themselves, if old enough).

Response:_____

Every two weeks we will have a family outing one evening, or weekend day, i.e., seeing a movie as a family, going out to dinner, going to the mall, playing games, going to the beach, etc.

Response:_____

Name calling and disrespect for another person is unacceptable and punishable.

Response:_____

We will all ask permission before taking/using another person's things.

Response:_____

Your room is off limits without your permission, with the exception of mom and dad.

Response:_____

Mom and dad will respect the need for privacy of the children and the children's rooms.

Response:_____

We will attend church and Sunday School weekly.
Response:_____

Each individual in the family will have assigned chores and times for completing them.

Response:_____

Other responses:_____

_____

_____

Home

What is your criteria for success for a home? This includes aspects of size, price, neighborhood, school system, and a number of other specific and concrete attributes. Evaluate these statements and determine how they might apply to you. Adjust them to meet your needs in the provided response space given. Be sure you are asking yourself the question, "On what am I basing my response?" For example, if you want to provide a $250,000 home for your family, and the bank says you can only afford an $85,000 home based on your salary, your criteria is flawed (even if your heart is in the right place) and you will be unsuccessful in providing a healthy response. Remember, we have moved from pathology to self-awareness. Allow that awareness to guide you in giving honest responses.

Everyone will have their own bedroom.

Response:_____

There will be a family/recreation room as well as a formal living room.

Response:_____

There will be an attached two-car garage with a workshop at least 10' x 10'

Response:_____

There will be 2 baths.

Response:_____

The bedrooms will be on the second floor along with the laundry room.

Response:_____

It will be on an acre of land with woods in the back.

Response:_____

The neighborhood will be multi-ethnic.

Response:_____

It will be no more than one mile from the schools.

Response:_____

The majority of families in the neighborhood will have children around the ages of our children.

Response:_____

Other responses:_____

_____

_____

_____

_____

Manhood / Womanhood

The concept of home was an easy one compared to the manhood or womanhood issues, because it is so much easier to be *concrete* in our responses (no pun intended). To deal with this issue takes a great deal of self-analysis and often-painful honesty regarding our capabilities and our limitations. Most of us don't like to consider that we have limitations, and therefore are not honest about what they are. We then place ourselves in untenable situations which frustrate, anger, depress, and ultimately defeat us. Look inward for this exercise. Remember what the "Little Prince" taught us—"it is only with the heart that one sees rightly, what is essential is invisible to the eye." I am combining manhood and womanhood and referring to the *androgynous* quality traits for this exercise. Those are the aspects of maleness and femaleness that each one of us carries with us, since no one is "completely male" or "completely female." *Androgyny* in no way addresses an individual's sexual preference. It does not refer to sexuality in any form. It only addresses the social attributes that society places on gender. For example, sensitivity to others is typically attributed to females, and is, therefore, considered to be a more *feminine* trait, although many men are highly sensitive. Being mechanical, or good with one's hands in fixing and building, is typically considered by our society to be a *masculine* trait despite the fact that many women are just as mechanical as men. Androgyny refers to a *balance* of those masculine and feminine traits within an individual's overall personality makeup. You can expand upon the criteria for success presented here with your specific gender needs.

I will be a person of integrity. I will use all of the information available to me at any given point in time, give honest assessment and feedback regarding that information, and make decisions that are considerate to the other parties involved. This involves removing "white lies" from our repertoire and at the same time being sensitive to the other individuals with whom we are involved. It involves feeling a response, then thinking about the response, then, finally, responding. It consists of having a foundational need to achieve a "win-win" scenario for all endeavors, understanding that if the situation culminates in a "win-lose" response, *the relationship loses.*

Response:_____

I will not place myself in situations that may compromise my integrity and honesty. If I find myself in that position, I will remove myself. I will guard against actions or appearances of impropriety in my social, sexual, business, spiritual, familial, financial, and relational life. This includes things like going to a casual dinner with a member of the opposite sex unaccompanied by your spouse, even if they are "just a friend," or sleeping in on Sunday morning out of convenience, rather than going to church, or planning to "adjust" your expense sheet to account for non-business expenses.

Response:_____

I will create and maintain healthy boundaries for myself, to protect myself and my family. I will do this understanding, to the best of my ability, both my capabilities and my limitations. This involves how much time I spend away from my home and family in non-work related activities like sports, hobbies, or helping other people. It also involves how much time I spend in work-related activities over and above the regular work schedule (bringing work home, for example). I will be willing to negotiate those factors with my spouse, and work toward a mutually satisfactory resolution.

Response:_____

I will attend at least one function involving my children (band concerts, sporting events, etc.) per week when my travel schedule permits it.

Response:_____

I will pray with each of my children daily, when I tuck them into bed, or I will call them to pray with them if I am on the road.

Response:_____

I will initiate devotions and prayer with my mate on a daily basis, or contact my mate daily when I am on the road.

Response:_____

I will read, pray, question, and explore ways to enhance myself as a spiritual individual on a daily basis.

Response:_____

I will challenge myself to admit and explore my fears and shortcomings, share those fears with someone close to me, and ask for support and accountability from that person on a weekly basis as I endeavor to overcome them.

Response:_____

I will challenge myself to learn something new about myself in every situation I encounter, and share that information with someone close to me.

Response:_____

Other responses:_____

_____

_____

It is easy to see that the criteria for success in the areas of manhood and womanhood are not easy to determine or grasp conceptually, not to mention behaviorally. As difficult as it may seem, however, it is still not as difficult as paying the ongoing consequences for not taking the time and devoting the energy to do it.

Sexuality

Sexuality is another one of those areas that creates some anxiety and difficulty for us to evaluate. One of my clients, when attempting to discuss some pertinent sexual issues, commented, "It's (sex) not something we want to talk about or think about, it's only something we want to *do,* and we want to do it right without talking about it or thinking about it." And, yet, sexuality is an area that often causes a great deal of angst in the relationship because we *don't* think or talk about it. Don't be surprised by your discomfort as you consider your thoughts on this subject. Instead, use your *honest acknowledgment of your discomfort* as a springboard for the growth and personal development of your sexual self.

I will become aware of my body and examine how it looks. I will do this for information, not for judgment. I will *not* grade or assess my body by any external factors (magazines, media, etc.), but instead *get to know it* and make "friends" with it, understanding that acceptance will allow me to change in ways that are healthy and positive for me.

Response:_____

I will be honest about the emotional sensations and the thought processes I am experiencing as I investigate my body. I will question the origin of those emotions and thoughts, and determine what messages I received in my family of origin that are the source of those emotions and thoughts. I will re-evaluate them in regard to their applicability to me at this point in my growth, and work to replace them and refocus if I find they have no place in my new criteria for success. This primarily addresses *guilt and anger,* the two phenomena most likely to impede healthy sexuality. They are common roadblocks to sexual fulfillment, and must be dealt with in order to grow. Remember, however, that the growth is a *process,* and that these issues will be considered one situation at a time.

Response:_____

I will read books and gather information about sexuality that is appropriate to my values and mores in order to expand my knowledge about healthy sexuality and sexual values. If I am unable to pursue this individually, or feel like I've hit a roadblock and cannot progress, I will get therapy from a qualified professional to help me progress.

Response:_____

I will share what I am learning, the emotions, knowledge, fears, experiences, sensations, and processes, with my mate, and solicit that information from my mate, so that our sexual relationship can be enhanced and provide mutual satisfaction. I will actively encourage my mate to share their sexual needs and wishes with me, to give me an opportunity to meet those needs. This is one of the most difficult of the sexual criteria for success because it requires *honesty, trust, mutuality, vulnerability, and consistency.* In this step we move slightly away from a personal criteria for success, and move into the realm of a relational criteria for success—what is going to work for *both* of you, and this takes many of the negotiating skills you will be learning in the next chapter. We will revisit this issue then.

Response:_____

Other responses:_____

_____

_____

_____

Church / God / Spirituality

This is a highly complex and personal issue, involving your individual relationship with God, something to which others may not be able to relate, or share the experience of. It also is another one of those issues about which we receive many messages from our family of origin, both positive and negative, verbal and nonverbal. Very often we receive mixed messages in which words are not matched by behavior. Evaluate these positions and adjust them to fit your personal relationship with God.

I choose to believe in a Divine power that is greater than I am and seek to have a personal relationship with God.

Response:_____

I choose to believe that it is only through this power that I can maintain any sense of balance in my life.

Response:_____

I believe that church membership, attendance, and participation is church activities is important for me and my family, and will encourage, support, and initiate involvement in those activities. In doing this, I will recognize that our lives also need activities unrelated to the church, and will work to create a balance of activities that are mutually acceptable to my mate and designed to meet the spiritual needs of our family that *we agree* are important. This may include youth group, church camps, choir, evening worship, Bible studies, etc.

Response:_____

I will support the church financially because I am spiritually and scripturally mandated to do so.

Response:_____

I will be honest about my *feelings and emotions* regarding the church, and evaluate the origin of those feelings to determine their historic significance to me. I will then decide on behaviors which will bring those emotions more into line with what I choose as a new and positive direction for my life. For example, children who were forced to go to church, regardless of and insensitive to whatever else might have been going on with them at the time, often carry a great deal of resentment toward the church into their adulthood. Being aware of that and understanding the source will enable that person to say, "Hey, no one is making me go to church now. I am doing this on the basis of my desire and my decision. I am in control of the situation!" As this occurs, the resentment toward church diminishes, and a new freedom of worship is possible.

Response:_____

An ethnically diverse church is important to me, and I will seek one out that has a similar belief system to my own.

Response:_____

I will get to know a variety of members from the church and stay away from cliques.

Response:_____

I will question God when I have questions. I will do this believing that I don't have to have all the answers, and realizing that much of my spiritual belief system is based on faith. I will speak to God often, be angry when I need to be angry, be happy when I am happy, and express whatever emotions I have to him. I will not withhold myself, my thoughts, my feelings, or my questions from God.

Response:_____

Other responses:_____

_____

_____

_____

Education

This might be both an individual issue and a family issue—what you expect and desire for yourself educationally, and what your expectations are of your children as they go through the educational process. Remember, we're looking for specific and behavioral criteria for success, not general themes.

Continuing my education as an adult is important for me, even if I've been away from school for a long time. To be successful I will go back to get my high school diploma / GED / bachelor's degree / master's degree / doctorate / certification / license, etc.

Response:_____

I will work with my mate to figure out how this can happen financially and in terms of time commitments and scheduling.

Response:_____

I believe, based on my experiences, that I am capable of getting no less that a "B" average in my classes, and will commit to do what it takes to accomplish that.

Response:_____

I realize that, due to the time demands schooling will place on me, I will have to give up some other endeavors (sports, hobbies, boards, etc.) to maintain a balance in my life. I will get feedback from my mate to determine how that can happen in such a way that will meet our mutual needs.

Response:_____

I will be clear with my mate about the specific and behavioral ways s/he can be most supportive of me as I go through this process (helping me study, reading my papers, quizzing me), and I will ask how I can be supportive of him/her through this process.

Response:_____

My children will attend all of their classes throughout school. The only exceptions will be illness, family events that take them away from school, and an occasional "mental-health holiday" that is negotiated between the parents and the child. Skipping school is not acceptable and the child will be accountable to the school for any consequences for unexcused absences.

Response:_____

Each class will be looked at independently, and success for that class will be determined by what is expected by the teacher and an honest effort (as determined by the parent) toward completing assignments and studying nightly.

Response:_____

Each child will be expected to participate in one extracurricular activity of their choice. The parents will be supportive financially and with their presence at functions when possible.

Response:_____

The parents will *actively pursue opportunities to affirm their children* throughout their educational process. This is the process of "Jiminy Cricket psychology," that is, accentuating the positive and eliminating the negative, as Jiminy Cricket instructed Pinnochio.

Response:_____

I will provide for my child whatever outside resources are available and within our means to assist them in producing the best possible overall results for their educational process. This may mean tutoring, afterschool help, special programs or seminars, etc.

Response:_____

Other responses:_____

_____

Work / Occupation

Before you begin this issue, review the messages you received about the issues of work and occupation from your family of origin. How were these messages played out by your father and mother? By their father and mother? Like so many other issues, if we are not aware of the messages we received, and the function of those messages in the family system, we are at risk to continue perpetuating messages and behaviors that have no place in the healthy lifestyles that we are attempting to put in place for ourselves and our families. The following statements may or may not exemplify what fits for you. Adjust them accordingly, so that they best reflect *your* position on the issues. Ask yourself these few questions:

1. What did my father (and/or mother) do for a living?
2. What do I know about how they came to do that particular job?
3. Did they pursue that job, or fall into it, and were they were prepared to do it?
4. Were they limited by lack of education, finances, or support to do the kind of job they wanted to do?
5. As you were growing up, did they make regular comments about wishing they were doing something else? If so, what else?
6. Are you doing the job they had commented that they wished they had had?

Now, having looked at those historic aspects of job and occupation, examine your criteria for success.

The purpose of my job is simply to provide enough money with which I can support my leisure time. What I do doesn't make a difference.

Response:_____

I must have a job that excites and challenges me on a regular basis. I cannot work in a "routine" atmosphere. The job must change continually to allow me to do new things.

Response:_____

What I do is of the utmost importance to me. I must believe in what I'm doing. This is so important that I am willing to make less money in order to have the opportunity to do it.

Response:_____

I will not allow my career to become more important than my marriage or family. I will look to my mate to give me feedback regarding whether or not my behavior indicates the secondary importance of my job in relationship to my family.

Response:_____

My job will have regular hours on which I can depend. I don't want to be involved in work past those hours. I want to leave work at work.

Response:_____

If what I am doing is meaningful to me, I am willing to do work over and above the schedule to accomplish the task, whether or not I am additionally compensated for it.

Response:_____

I need to be involved in a job where I can see the finished product in order to give me a sense of accomplishment. I can't work on only one piece of a project and be content.

Response:_____

I need to work with other people to stimulate me. Working alone bores me and I get easily distracted.

Response:_____

I need to work alone because other people distract and irritate me. I need to be given a project and allowed to complete that project using my own processes, not a process someone else has developed for me.

Response:_____

I need my father / mother / wife / husband / to be proud of me for what I do for a living, and I would change jobs to make that happen.

Response:_____

I want my children to follow in my footsteps, and have the same type of career that I do.

Response:_____

I would never want my children to do the kind of work that I do.

Response:_____

Other responses:_____

_____

_____

_____

We can see that developing a specific and behavioral criteria for success is rather daunting, but a necessary part of creating a new and healthy lifestyle. I encourage you to go back over your answers to the BIAS-R and, with each issue, take the time and energy to begin creating your "healthy lifestyle road map" by developing those criteria which will help you achieve success—according to *your* new working definition of the term.

In the next chapter we will bring the personal criteria for success into your relationship, and concentrate on healthy and appropriate methods of getting your needs met, and on meeting the needs of your mate. The foundational principles of healthy coupleship will be examined, and you'll need to bring your awareness of what you've been learning about you along for the ride!

Shadowchaser

GO BACK OVER YOUR RESPONSES IN DETERMINING EACH AREA'S CRITERIA FOR SUCCESS. AT THE END OF EACH SEC-TION CONSIDER THE FEELINGS YOU EXPERIENCED WHILE REVIEWING. WERE THERE FEELINGS OF CONTENTMENT? JOY? RESIGNATION? FRUSTRATION? ANGER? EVALUATE HOW THOSE RESPONSES AND SUBSEQUENT ANSWERS HAVE IMPACTED YOU SPECIFICALLY AND BEHAVIORALLY IN THOSE AREAS, AS WELL AS IN YOUR MARRIAGE AND FAMILY.

CHAPTER 7

A Matter of Needs:
The Art of Being Appropriately Selfish

"If someone forces you to go one mile,
go with them two miles.
Give to the one who asks you,
and do not turn away
from the one who wants
to borrow from you."
–Matthew 5:41-42 NIV

"One of the weaknesses of our age
is our apparent inability
to distinguish our
needs from our greeds."
–Don Robinson

Chloë must have been about four years old when she came up to our bedroom several hours after she had been put to bed. It was dark, and something must have frightened her because she was crying softly and clutching "Pooh" and her blanket.

"Chloë, what's wrong?" her mother asked.

"I don't want to sleep downstairs. I'm *scared* and I'm *lonely.*"

"What do you *need* Chloë?"

"I need *you*, because you're my mommy."

It was as simple as that. Chloë was doing what she needed to do in order to pursue the needs she had at the moment. Even at four years old she understood the basic dynamic that there is a certain strength in the relationship, and that the relationship has at its core the ability to meet the needs of the individuals involved more often than not.

This chapter deals with the all-important issue of learning how to take care of yourself both in and out of relationships. It is true that the better an individual is able to pursue their needs, the healthier they will become. And the healthier they become, the more they have to offer in a healthy relationship. This chapter also discusses the need for a high degree of *mutuality* in healthy relationships. This is the glue that helps us keep our focus forward, instead of backward into our old patterns of thinking and behaving.

Relationships are typically at the core of all sorts of jokes and stories. On a recent trip, I encountered several quips which I felt portrayed the diversity of attitudes regarding relationships. Two bumper stickers read:

"The more I know women, the more I love my truck."
And:
"If they can send one man to the moon, why not send all of them?"

Those attitudes aside, there were two quotes that got my attention in a positive sense regarding healthy marriages. The first, by Harold Nicholson, read, "The great secret of successful marriage is to treat all disasters as incidents and none of the incidents as disasters."

And, finally, my favorite, a quote from Flora Davis.

"Almost all married people fight, although many are ashamed to admit it. Actually a marriage in which no quarreling at all takes place may well be the one that is dead or dying from emotional under-nourishment. If you care, you probably fight."

I think she has it right. Healthy relationships experience the full and complete range of emotions. The emotional "salsa" is part of what fuels the marriage and keeps it alive. It is handling that salsa in a mutually acceptable way that keeps the marriage healthy. Let's go over some of the principles involved in the art of being appropriately selfish and developing healthy relationships.

1. Relationships are based on needs

This principle refers to the fact that all relationships have at their core a need to be in a relationship! If we didn't have needs, we probably wouldn't be in relationships, because they are such a pain, not to mention an incredible amount of work. And beyond the need to be in a relationship, every issue that arises in the relationship is also based on needs. When a relationship is working well it is because the *mutual* needs of the individuals involved are being met as much as is possible. When a relationship is not working well, I never have to dig very far down to find a pile of unmet needs.

Sometimes the needs do not manifest themselves immediately and require some searching to get below the issue to find out what they are. Here's an example:

I have always had a deep need to be involved in activities that have an "edge" to them—something to get the adrenaline pumping and the blood surging. I have enjoyed activities like fencing, motor-cross racing, hydroplane racing, surfing, scuba diving, walking out on the ice floes of Lake Michigan and exploring the ice caves, mountain biking, jet skiing, flying, and sky diving.

It wasn't too long after we had gotten married that Colette came to me with a need, although at first glance I saw it as an assault on my personhood!

"I need you to stop doing the things you're doing as hobbies, she said.

"Say what...?"

"I need you to not do all of those kinds of things you've been doing because they're too dangerous."

"You've got to be kidding! Give up my stuff? You knew I was doing all of this stuff when you married me. What's the big deal now?"

"That's the point. You're married now and you have someone to think about beside yourself. The things you do are dangerous and I don't want to lose you."

"Absolutely not! Out of the question! It's not fair to marry me and then expect me to give up the things that are important to me. I haven't asked you to give up *knitting,* and that's a pretty lame thing that *you* do."

And I walked away.

I was really stretching at this point, but I couldn't figure out at all where she was coming from. I was feeling manipulated, and she was feeling misunderstood, unheard, and not taken seriously. Not bad for a couple of professionals in the mental health field!

I made several mistakes right off the top in that conversation.

First, I didn't ask her to clarify and describe what she meant, *specifically and behaviorally,* when she was asking me to give up my hobbies. I immediately processed that information as, "she's asking me to give up my life!" I reacted strongly to it.

Second, I got off track from the issue and started after her. How could *she* do this to me? What could *she* be thinking? Why was *she* manipulating me. And I pursued the conversation from that point, attacking the knitting that she does and making the argument about her.

Third, I bailed out on the conversation. Taking a time-out to regroup is sometimes a good idea if the emotional intensity of the situation is getting too near the boiling point. But that's not what I did. I bailed out of the conversation because I didn't want to hear anything else she had to say...because if I stayed, I might *lose*.

Unfortunately, this is a very common type of argument in a relationship. We make it emotional, attack the other person, get off issue, and before we know it, we've made a tremendous mess out of it. And both parties crawl away to their neutral corners and either come at it again later, deny that a problem exists, or stuff it—at which point it becomes another brick in the wall between them in the relationship.

The good news is that later I went back to Colette and apologized for the way I handled the situation.

"Help me understand where you're coming from," I asked.

Those first three words are incredibly valuable in resolving issues and getting to the needs. They let the other person know that you really want to hear what they have to say, because it will help resolve the issue.

"I'm just afraid. I don't want anything to happen to you, and I'm afraid something will with the kinds of things you like doing."

"What do you need to become more *comfortable* with what I do? Is there anything that I can do that would make at least some of these things more acceptable?"

She thought about it from that perspective.

"If you just wouldn't do the immediately life-threatening things, like motorcycles and hydroplanes, then I could live with some of it. And, if I knew that you were taking every safety precaution in the things you did, I could feel more comfortable about some of it, too."

Then *I* thought about it from *her* perspective.

"I need you to know that I don't have some death wish like you might think. I can give up the motorcycles and hydroplanes, and what I need from you is that you will trust me that when I do the other things I do, I *do and will use* all of the safety precautions. I'll be glad to tell you what they are, if you wish. What do *you* need to be okay with that?"

The conversation continued until we could both look at each other and say, "I can live with that." At that point, and not before, the situation was resolved.

Resolving issues is not an easy task because it is very difficult to be personally objective, and the more emotional we become regarding the issue, the less opportunity we have to ensure that our emotions won't cloud our objectivity, sensibility, and confuse the issue even further.

There are two tools that are invaluable in assessing needs in any given situation. The tools are simple in theory and simple to use, but often part of a difficult process. We'll examine that difficulty momentarily. First, let's examine the tools.

Tool #1

Understanding that at the core of every issue are numerous unmet needs, at the point *where the issue is raised,* ask this question: *"What do you need from me right now?"*

This is the quickest route to resolution. If we immediately go for the needs, we diminish the possibilities of the situation escalating emotionally to the point where resolution becomes dynamically impossible.

If it's that simple, then why doesn't everyone do it now? There are two reasons for that. First, in our culture and as a result of our lifestyles, there is typically an underlying layer of *paranoia* in each of us. We truly believe that the other person is out to get us! Therefore, if we are attacked, or even if we are not attacked, but perceive that an attack is imminent or currently happening, our natural and automatic response is to *attack back.* An example of our paranoid tendency toward miscommunication might look like this:

"Honey, you said you would take the garbage out last night and you didn't. The garbage men came and went this morning, and our can is full."

"Yeah, well you told me you would have my shirts ironed this morning, and they weren't either. I had to wear the same one I wore yesterday. So, don't talk to me about garbage."

Well, hmmm… it *all* sounds like garbage to me. The chances of that conversation ending up on a positive note are negligible. Let's replay it in a different format.

"Honey, you said you would take the garbage out last night and you didn't. The garbage men came and went this morning and our can is full."

"I'm sorry. It totally slipped my mind. I was running late this morning and tore out of the garage without even thinking that today was Monday and the garbage men were coming. What do you need from me right now?"

The answer would probably have been something like, "Nothing, just please remember next week," or, "Could you maybe take a couple of bags to the dumpster at work so we could get a few more in our can?" or something to that effect. The two most common complaints about communication that I hear in my office are:

"He (or she) doesn't listen to me. I never feel like I'm being heard." And:

"He (or she) doesn't take me seriously. It's like what I say doesn't really matter."

In addition, we aren't used to communicating about our needs. In our culture, the pursuit of one's own needs has been given a rather derogatory label—*selfish*—and no one wants to carry around that reputation. When we were children and had a special toy, and Johnny came over to play (Johnny the Terrible, who had broken our toys previously) and we didn't want him to play with that toy, we were told, "Stop being so selfish. Now, let Johnny play with that toy." Or when we were really hungry and there was one pork chop left on the plate, we didn't dare ask for it or take it, because when we had done that previously we had been branded selfish. Or when we didn't want to play with our little sisters because they had been making us absolutely crazy, and we barricaded ourselves in our rooms with the stereo blasting through our headphones, we were called selfish.

The Don Robinson quote at the opening of this chapter bears repeating at this point: "*One of the weaknesses of our age is our apparent inability to distinguish our **needs** from our **greeds**.*" It is the task of the parent to help the child understand the difference, and a grievous error in parenting is that all too often that does not happen. But then, how could it? Their parents didn't teach them, either! As we are better able to assess our needs and distinguish them from our whims, wishes, desires, fantasies, and greeds, we will then feel much more comfortable (over time) in pursuing those things which *are* legitimate needs in any given situation.

Tool #2

This particular tool has two parts, and they must be part of the *same package*. To use one part and not the other can render the package ineffective at best, and at worst give the appearance of "selfishness" or that the other person is not part of the equation. The two parts are these:

"Here's what I need from you right now in regard to this situation."

"What do *you* need to meet *my* need?"

This is the *opening* volley in a round of negotiations that is designed for one purpose, and one purpose only—to create a *win—win* resolution to the situation. It demonstrates our ability to be honest in a situation, push past our paranoia, make ourselves vulnerable, and put our needs out there FIRST. Why is that so important? The reason lies in two dictums of communication. And while these two items present a negative aspect to communication in the midst of describing a positive tool, it is necessary to describe them to increase our awareness of what can go wrong if we don't possess the knowledge of how to overcome them. Those dictums are:

1. Information is power

2. The one who gives the least *(communication)* controls the relationship.

Let's explore that for a moment. Information as power is probably not news to anyone. The more we know, the better we feel, and the better decisions can be made based on that information. But what about the other one—giving the least and controlling the relationship? Really, it makes perfect sense. If I can find out everything there is about you, and not let you know very much about me, then I can use that information to my advantage to control the relationship. Remember—in relationships we all tend to have that paranoid streak running just beneath the surface. This is especially true when it comes to questions. When someone asks a question, we sometimes wonder why they were asking the question, and would perhaps answer the question differently based on their reason for asking the question in the first place. Realizing our tendency, the goal is to *push through* our fears, and entertain the questions as an effort on the part of the other person to get to know us better and truly connect in a positive way.

A husband and wife came to see me for marital counseling, asking for assistance in their communication processes. Both had been married before and they had just completed their first year of marriage. But the communication process was flawed and it was creating a great deal of anxiety and stress in the relationship. Unable to sort through the issue themselves, they decided it was time for outside intervention. The problem? He wouldn't give her a straight answer to her questions. Regardless of the question, his response was likely to be one of these:

"I don't care."

"Whatever you want."

"It doesn't matter to me."

"Your decision."

"Do what you need to do."

"Anything's okay by me."

The wife lamented, "I know he's got opinions. I just don't know how to get to them. He was this way when we were dating, too, but I thought it would change after we got married and knew each other better. But it hasn't—and it's making me crazy!"

The husband admitted that it was making him crazy, too, but he couldn't figure out why he was so reluctant to answer her questions. "It's not that I don't have an answer, but I get all nervous and afraid to give it. Maybe I just don't want it to be the wrong answer." When I asked what would happen if it *were* the wrong answer he said, "Probably nothing. I don't know what the problem is..."

The couple was really feeling stuck and defeated by the faulty communication hookup. It wasn't until we began to talk about family-of-origin issues, and the communication styles used in his family, that he began to understand. "My mother and father used to ask me questions all the time. And they *knew,* or at least they thought they knew, the answers *they* wanted to hear, regardless of whether or not it was the right answer. And if I didn't guess what the answer was they wanted to hear—I got cuffed along side the head, or grounded, or punished in some other way. So I learned the art of the *non-answer.* And my ex-wife was the mistress of the manipulative question. She had a real high need to control the relationship. We both did. And our marriage got to be one big power struggle. But one of the ways she controlled was by the use of questions. She would ask a question like, "Oh, look. This movie is playing downtown. Would you like to go see that movie?" If I said no, she would say, 'You always get your way. Why don't you ever want to do anything with me.' If I said yes, she would probably say something like, 'You know, I think that's just about the most stupid movie that's ever been made. I don't know why anyone would want to go see that movie.'"

He recalled another instance when he and his ex-wife were driving downtown at dinner time. "Where would you like to go to eat?" she asked. "I'm hungry for a steak," he replied. Her response: "Why do we always have to go where *you* want to eat. I wish once in a while you would consider what I want to do."

What this young man learned very early in life was that he could expect questions to be used against him in a variety of ways, and that his emotional survival depended upon his ability to avoid giving answers to those questions. He also was able to relate that this same hesitancy to respond had a negative impact on him in other relationships and at work. "I got passed over for a promotion because my supervisor told the boss that I didn't have an opinion about anything, so how could I run a crew?"

The solution occurred on two levels. One of them he had to learn *one situation at a time*, was that not everyone was out to get him, especially his wife, who simply wanted to know what he thought and felt about matters. This required him to step out of his comfort zone and become vulnerable, risking that his wife would treat his answers sensitively and appropriately. This would only happen over time, as she consistently demonstrated that he could trust her sensitivity. And, two, his wife learned that *behind every question is a statement, and to give the statement before asking the question automatically reduces defensiveness, and increases the potential to get an honest answer.* In learning to give her input first, she made *herself* vulnerable—an open invitation for him to do the same thing. For example, instead of asking him, "Where would you like to go for dinner?" she learned how to share with him, "I'm sort of hungry for Chinese takeout tonight. What are you hungry for?" In this way she was presenting him with the opportunity to participate in the win—win scenario we spoke of earlier; to get both of their needs met in the transaction.

This also is a very powerful tool that can be used with children. I have encountered situations when an upset child could not tell me what was wrong, but they could tell me what they "needed" at the time. Teaching your children how to use this tool also increases their ability to negotiate in healthy ways and get more of their needs met as they progress through life. However, teaching your children this tool can have some interesting side effects.

Nathan was about 17 when I got my new Jeep. It was great. Deep blue with a black soft-top, and a really good stereo system with front and rear speakers. It was a birthday present from my wife and I loved it. One Thursday afternoon Nathan began hanging around like adolescents do when they have something on their mind.

"What's up, Nate, you look like a man on a mission."

"Well, Dad, I've been thinking..."

I have learned over time that the parent is usually in deep trouble when their child begins a conversation with "I've been thinking..."

"Yes...?"

"Well, you know I'm going camping this weekend with Carl."

"Yes...?"

"And, well,...I've been thinking...it would really be cool if you'd let me take your Jeep. *What do you **need** to be okay with that?*"

I'd been had! He had used the tool skillfully, and as much as I wanted to say no, it wasn't a yes or no question. Had he asked, "Dad, can I take your Jeep this weekend?" that would have been easy.

"No, you can't." End of discussion.

But he had expressed his *need* (actually a whim disguised as a need), and then went after what I needed to meet his need. And he did it well!

"Make sure it's clean and full of gas when you get back," I growled. And he was on his way.

There are really only two situations in which the two tools we've described here will not work. First, *it will not work if someone is not being honest about what they need.* In order for the tools to be effective, they require us to present how we really think and feel about issues, and what our needs really are. Second, *it will not work if the issue at hand is non-negotiable.* Non-negotiable issues typically have something to do with legal, ethical, or moral subjects, and we don't tend to bring them up in the first place if we are interested in having a healthy relationship. Nevertheless, they do come up from time to time.

I once had a young couple in my office who were having some serious marital problems with commitment. I explained the "needs" tools to them, gave them several examples, and asked them to "try it out" while they were in my office. The man turned to his wife and said, "What I need to get along in this relationship with you is for it to be okay with you that I go out and have relationships with other women, too. What do you need to be okay with that?"

Right technique! Wrong stance! Her answer was a classic one and I've never forgotten it. She turned to him, smiled, and said, *"Not in this lifetime!"* It was a non-negotiable issue, and inappropriate in any healthy relationship. Their marriage self-destructed shortly after that.

Additionally, there are three extremely important questions which must be addressed by both individuals in the relationship when considering a decision or resolution to an issue.

1. How will this decision (or action) impact me short- and long-term?

2. How will this decision impact my mate?

3. How will this decision impact the relationship?

The answers to questions 2 and 3 are best answered in discussion with our mates. After all, why guess? Question 1 can be stated in such a way as to challenge your personal responsibility, integrity, and desire to make decisions that are in the best interest of healthy coupleship. The restating of the question looks like this: *"Is what I'm about to do or say going to demonstrate my commitment to the relationship, enhance the well-being of my mate, and ultimately be to the glory of God?"*

If the answer is *no*—don't do it!

If the answer is *maybe*—don't do it!

The only time action should occur is if you can answer an unequivocal *yes* to the question.

Margaret and Harris had been invited by another couple to dinner and a classical organ concert. Margaret, who received the invitation, made a decision based on her relationship with Harris that he would not enjoy the concert. She accepted the invitation for herself, and declined for Harris.

The night before the concert Harris confronted her with her actions. "Whether or not I would have chosen to go is not the issue. It would have been nice had you given *me* the option of telling you I was not interested in going." As Margaret related this story to me she added, "What that smacked of to me was inconsideration and thoughtlessness on my part. I knew neither of these was true because I *am* a thoughtful and considerate person. What I had done, however, was taken the responsibility away from him, and dishonored the relationship at the time. I had done this previously, and he had asked me, 'Did you take me to love or to raise? I've been raised once and don't need to be again.'" Harris was pointing out that "Mother Margaret" (as she noted her tendencies from time to time) needed to focus more attention on mutuality in the relationship.

Let's continue our examination of addressing our needs and the needs of others in the relationship.

2. Before we can present our needs we must be able to define and understand them in behavioral terms.

As we did when we examined our criteria for success, it is necessary in our needs assessment to define our needs in terms of specific behaviors. This is crucial because each of us tends to speak different emotionally descriptive languages. For example—when I say, *"I need you to love me more,"* I know exactly what that means to me. I can visualize it in my mind, I can feel what it would be like, I understand what the impact would be on me, and I have an expectation that when I tell you that I need you to love me more, you will know *exactly, specifically, and behaviorally what I am referring to!*

Fat chance!

Because when I say, *"I need you to love me more,"* you go through exactly the same procedure. You can visualize it in your mind, you can feel what it would be like, you might understand what the impact would be on you, and have a similar *expectation* that I know what it means to you that it means to me. Confused? You certainly would be if we left it right there. If I am going to express a need to you, I have an *obligation* to present that need to you in definable terms that we both understand.

"I need you to love me more" translates into—
"I am a very affectionate person."
"I require lots of physical contact."
"I need six or seven hugs a day."
"I need us to kiss and hug before we part and when we get back together."
"I need sexual intimacy at least three times a week."
*"I need **you** to initiate physical contact at least a couple of times a day."*
*"I need you to **tell me** you love me at least once a day."*
"I need you to call me at least once a day when you're on the road."
"When we're together, in the car, or at the mall, or in the movies, I want to hold hands most of the time."

Wow! Quite a difference from "I need you to love me more." With the behavioral description, we have defined the concept in such a way that it leaves the least amount of room for misinterpretation, and gives the *most opportunity* for our needs to be met.

Let's take a look at some other potential translations and clarifications on some common issues in relationships.

Need expressed: *"I need you to be more of a father."*
Translation: "By the time you get home, I've had it with the kids. I've been with them all day and I really need a break. I don't need you to completely take over for me, and I don't need to completely bail out on you. If you see them doing something wrong, I need you to correct them, and not wait for me to do it. I need you to make sure they're washed up and ready when dinner is prepared. And at dinner, please help me get them to eat. At bedtime, I would appreciate it if we could make it a couple affair, getting them washed up, pajamas on, teeth brushed, in bed, and stories and prayers done. Doing that together would make it a much easier task and allow us to have a little more time together before *I* collapse in bed."

Need expressed: *"I need you to be more responsible with the checkbook."*
Translation: "When I balanced the checkbook over the past three months there were $400 worth of checks and ATM withdrawals that were not recorded by you. It is a tremendous headache for me to have to fig-

ure out where the problems in the checkbook are anyway, so I really need your help with this. If I am going to continue to handle the balancing of the checkbook, I need you to commit to be more diligent in recording your transactions."

Need expressed: *"I need you to pick up after yourself."*
Translation: "When you use something and leave it out, or take your clothes off and drop them wherever you are, I feel like you don't respect me or appreciate the job I do to keep our home picked up and looking nice. I don't mind picking up most of the time, but it would be really helpful to me if you would at least be aware of when you do this, and make an attempt at putting things away and dealing with your clothes. This is especially important to me on Wednesday evening, because I clean the house on Thursday morning, and I need to have things in some order. What do *you* need to help me out in this way?"

The last translation is an example of the complete package. The need is expressed, described, and then the needs of the other individual are solicited in an effort to achieve the Win-Win scenario.

One other factor we need to address in regard to effective communication techniques for presenting our needs is the factor of *personality differences,* and how those differences impact communication.

When Nathan, my oldest son, was small, if he was out of line in some way, all I had to do was give him *the look.* You know the one. It's the same one your father gave you and my father gave me. And with Nathan, that's all it took. One shot of *the look* in his direction and he fell right back into line—at least temporarily.

Then Collin came along. When he got out of line in some way, and I gave him *the look—he gave it back to me.* Not in a disrespectful way, but in more of a "Wow, that's a funny face...I wonder if I can make a face like that." With Collin I was forced to find verbal ways to bring him back on track.

When Nicholas came along, I had great hope that *the look* would work with him. After all, it's so easy. If only the kids would cooperate. But, it didn't work with him, either. When I gave him *the look,* he commented on it. "Look, Mommy, Daddy's making that funny face again. Do it again, Daddy, please..." And it would be all Colette could do to keep a straight face. Like Collin, with Nicholas I was forced to change my approach to a verbal and behavioral one.

I thought I just about had it figured out when Chloë came along. After all, girls couldn't be *that much different.* You know, I've advocated in my practice for years that there is nothing on the face of the earth that can make a person feel more inadequate than being in the role of parent. And Chloë proved me right. When Chloë got a bit off track, and I gave her *the look* to bring her back, *she burst into tears, buried her face in her hands, and ran into her room.* Now I had an *additional* problem.

Each one of the children has a very different personality as well as a very different process with which they communicate. And the language I had to develop with each one was very different and very necessary if I was ever going to communicate effectively with them. The same is true in marriages. We each speak a different language, and if we enter the relationship simply expecting that the other person is going to speak our language, we diminish the opportunities for effective communication as well as diminishing our opportunities to affirm and honor that other person.

When I am out speaking about communication I often use the example of Colette speaking Russian. She had a minor in Russian in college. "How many of you speak Russian," I'll ask. It's usually a safe bet because not many of the audiences I speak to have a background in Russian language. I then go on to say, "Colette would like to speak with you in the hallway after I'm finished. She has some important information to share with you. She's going to be speaking Russian exclusively, so be prepared." I then ask them what they think the experience would be like for them if that were to occur. I get words like "frustrating," "exasperating," "unintelligible," "I wouldn't put up with it," or "I'd tell her to speak English or I am outta here!"

My point exactly!

If we are truly interested in getting our points across to the individuals with whom we have close and intimate relationships, *the language they speak becomes more important than the language we may be comfortable with **if we have the option!*** This becomes critical, because sometimes we *don't* have the option, and then the miscommunication is going to be consistent and debilitating unless we can get a translator to help us understand, interpret, and learn the other person's verbal, emotional, or personality language. That translator is most often a therapist, and the therapy becomes necessary at the point the individuals look at each other and say, "Nothing we've tried is bringing our communication in line with each other. We need help." Through that process, the couple will hopefully get the "language lessons" they need to be an effective and healthy communicating couple.

3. Before we can present our needs, we must be able to determine their "functional foundation"

The functional foundation of needs refers to their point of origin, and what created them as needs in the first place. Freud is *credited* with saying, "Sometimes a cigar is just a cigar," and the same is true with needs. (No, not that needs are the same as cigars.) Sometimes a need is just a need, and there is no functional foundation. On the other hand, there are some needs that carry with them the sort of intensity that surpasses what we might call our ordinary, day-to-day, garden-variety needs. Those needs we pursue with much more passion, and getting them met, in some cases, becomes non-negotiable. They *must* be met if we are to exist in the relationship. It is *these* needs to which I am referring when I speak of functional foundation. Here are some examples of the needs and the potential originating phenomena which created them.

Need	Functional foundation
We must go to church every Sunday. =	We were punished severely if we missed church for any reason. I *still* fear not going and being punished.
I have to be with you all the time. =	My parents would leave for hours at a time when I was young, and never tell us where they were going, and we were always scared. I'm afraid you'll abandon me too!
I need to be in charge of the checkbook, and I have to know we have a cushion of money at all times. =	My dad never let my mother see the checkbook, and he spent money irresponsibly. There always were creditors coming to the door or phoning. It was horrible, shaming, and embarrassing.
After we have fought, and then resolved the issues, I need to be held by you and reassured that everything is going to be okay. =	My folks would punish us by withdrawing, not speaking to us, or not acknowledging that we even existed. It was like we were dead.

With these examples it is much easier to see why these particular needs would carry more emotional weight than some of the others. When both people understand where the needs originate from, and the role they played in the family of origin *as well as in the marriage,* empathy and acceptance are much more possible.

4. We must learn how to effectively solicit the needs of the other individual and, as much as is possible, meet them

There are several traits that I consider to be crucial to being a healthy mate. And as you read these, please keep in mind that healthy couple-ship is predicated upon *mutuality.* **Both individuals share these traits.**
They are:

1. An overwhelming desire to meet the needs of their mate.

2. An ability to tolerate ambiguity, and accept things even if they can't understand them.

3. A willingness to negotiate any issue that arises in the relationship to mutual satisfaction.

4. Stamina to work at resolution until a mutually acceptable conclusion is achieved.

5. The desire to learn the language of the other individual and the willingness to use it consistently *for the sake of coupleship.*

6. The ability to realize that unless a solution culminates in a Win—Win scenario, no solution has been reached.

I often explain it to folks this way. If I'm smart, really smart, I'm going to do everything in my power to make sure my wife's needs are met. And I'm going to do this if for no other reason than a very selfish one. And that reason is: *If her needs are met, as much as is possible, she is going to be a much happier camper. And, if she's a much happier camper, **who** do you think is going to get the benefit of that?*

We call that kind of attitude (not the selfish one, but the willingness and desire to meet her needs) *"servant leadership."* And in terms of how a relationship functions, I have seen an interesting pattern develop as a result of servant leadership: *I never have encountered a marriage where, if the man presented himself as the servant leader, that the wife didn't gladly submit to his authority.*

The reason seems relatively simple. In that type of relationship, that woman has *experienced consistently over time* that what that man does will address her needs, will be designed for her fulfillment, provision, and protection, and that every decision that he makes will have her best interests in mind. Not at the expense of his own thoughts, or feelings, or needs, but, rather, placing them *all* in the pot, and determining together how they can get the maximum number of their mutual needs met. This is not describing perfection in our mates either. It *is*, however, defining a relationship where the commitment is to continue to head in the right direction—together! This defines coupleship!

Now that we have examined the mechanisms needed to create healthy relationships, it's time to move on to what is necessary to raise healthy children. In our next chapter we will focus on our children—our futures, and what we can do to assist our children in perpetuating the healthy lifestyles we are working so hard to achieve.

Shadowchaser

IT IS IMPORTANT TO EXAMINE SPECIFICALLY AND BEHAVIORALLY WHAT OUR NEEDS ARE IN EVERY PART OF OUR LIVES. IT IS EQUALLY IMPORTANT TO SOLICIT, BE AWARE OF, AND PURSUE THE NEEDS OF THOSE PEOPLE WHO ARE IMPORTANT TO US. LET'S EXAMINE SOME OF THOSE AREAS AND CONSIDER THE NEEDS.

LOVE: WHAT WILL IT LOOK LIKE, SPECIFICALLY AND BEHAVIORALLY, IF I AM BEING LOVED IN THE WAY THAT IS MOST MEANINGFUL TO ME?

FINANCES: WHAT DO I NEED TO FEEL SECURE FINANCIALLY?

SPIRITUALITY: WHAT, SPECIFICALLY AND BEHAVIORALLY, ENHANCES MY GOD CONNECTION?

FRIENDSHIPS: WHAT DO I NEED TO FEEL FULFILLED AND SATISFIED IN MY FRIENDSHIPS?

GO OVER EACH OF THESE AREAS WITH YOUR MATE AND COMPARE ANSWERS.

CHAPTER 8

Children of Hope—
Children of Light

"My son, if your heart is wise,
then my heart will be glad;
my inmost being will rejoice
when your lips speak what is right."
–Proverbs 23: 15-16

"We are surrounded with
insurmountable opportunities."
–Pogo

"In every child that is born,
under no matter what the circumstances,
and of no matter what the parents,
the potentiality of the human race is born again;
and in him, too, once more, and of each of us,
our terrific responsibility towards human life. . ."
–James Agee

When Collin was about four years old, and Nathan was eight, we lived in a tract development in a small community in the East Bay near San Francisco. It was one of those tracts where every house was a mirror image of the others, making them indistinguishable one from the other except for the colors they were painted. Our neighbors were a very nice professional couple who had wanted two children, and the second one was triplets! Two boys and a girl who were just about Nathan's age. Although Collin was the youngest of the group, they typically played well together and spent lots of time at each other's houses. Nathan attended the public school, which was right across the street, and Collin attended a Christian preschool across town. We were pleased with the preschool and with what he was learning. And Collin would come home every Friday excited to share the different Bible verse he had learned over the course of the week.

On one particular Friday, I happened to be working at home in my office which faced the street in front of the house. Nathan, Collin, and the triplets were playing with a ball in the front yard, chasing one another around and having a great time. At one point, Nathan had the ball and was tripped by one of the triplets. It didn't appear to be intentional, but, nevertheless, Nathan went down in a heap and began to cry. Collin, who had observed this entire episode, thought for a few brief moments, walked over to the offending triplet, and with a solid right hook to the nose dropped the young man to the ground. The young triplet looked up, astonished!

"What did you do that for?" he yelled, as he checked his nose for blood. Finding none, he rose and stared down at Collin, "What did you hit me for?"

Collin put his hands on his hips, looked the boy in the eye, and said, "Because Jesus said, 'We must be kind to one another,' and you weren't kind to my brother!"

And while I didn't approve of his methods, I had to give Collin a tremendous amount of credit for his tenacity, his willingness to stand up for what he believed—and that he had learned, and applied, his Bible verse *very well*. In fact, he was learning all of his lessons well.

Too well...

I had to ask myself the question, "Where had he learned that aggression would solve his problems? What had he seen and experienced from me, as his male role model, that was influencing him on his day to day journey in his short little life? Or, was he, in fact, learning what he needed from me, or some other source? After all, I was on the road a lot. *What was he learning?*"

The goal is simple: To teach our children everything they need to know in order to be the absolute best individuals they can be, learning from our mistakes without having to repeat them, being loyal to our healthy traits, and disloyal in inoffensive ways to our dysfunctional patterns. To understand the concept of homeostasis and resist it when it interferes with their healthy direction. To not be overly influenced by family-of-origin issues and to distinguish which behaviors are healthy and which are not.

A simple goal.
A simple concept.
*An **impossible** task...*

As we consider the difficult task of producing healthy children in an unhealthy world, we must grasp one small ray of hope in this statement that we referred to earlier in this book:

It's not about perfection, it's about direction

It is our job to use all of the information *we* have learned about our past, our families of origin, the functions of our unhealthy behaviors in the family system, how we did our part to maintain the homeostasis in the family system. It is also our job to use all of this information in order to present our children with the support and the opportunity to perhaps do it differently, to do it in a way that preserves the uniqueness and special qualities of the personality God has given them.

In this final chapter we will examine six factors in raising healthy children. It is by no means a complete list, but will assist you in beginning the process, or at least examining your own current process, of creating in your children the light and hope for their future.

1. We must actively pursue opportunities to affirm our children

Self-esteem is the fuel that drives our children to dare dreaming their dreams, pursuing their visions, and performing the great things for which they were created. And our affirmations on an honest and consistent basis are our contributions to "filling their tanks." It is not enough that we acknowledge performance when it is brought to our attention, for that does nothing to separate us as parents from teachers, coaches, or spectators in life who appreciate and congratulate a good show. As parents, our task is far more frequent, specific, directed, and necessary. It is from the parents that the affirmations mean the most to the child and have the greatest impact over the long term.

I watched bits and pieces of the Summer Olympics from Atlanta. The broadcasts included many up close and personal segments showing how the athletes rose through the ranks to walk among the *best athletes in the world!* In every story there were pictures of parents coaching, encouraging, pushing, holding accountable, loving, crying, celebrating—and affirming. We all have read the horror stories of the parents who *pushed* their children in athletics to fulfill their *own needs*. And of the parents whose sole reason for supporting an endeavor with a child was for their own vicarious pleasure and satisfaction. But, that's not what we're talking about here. We're talking about parents who have helped their children *celebrate* themselves, their accomplishments, their unique gifts and qualities—their personhood. *And,* in watching the athletes from the United States who had the largest contingencies of family present and available to support them, after each stellar performance was completed, their eyes immediately focused on the grandstand to find that parent or parents who had stood by and affirmed them. One boxer, in particular, cried after a loss. His comment, "I just didn't want to let my mother down." One fencer, whose mother sacrificed to get him involved in the sport, credits her with saving his life. Most of the friends he grew up with in his neighborhood were in prison or dead. There were the Greco-Roman wrestlers who, after the match, immediately went to the stands and hugged their fathers and cried with them. And the one who took off his medal and hung it around his father's neck. *These athletes did not grow up in a vacuum. They did not grow up in a punitive, judgmental, critical, demeaning atmosphere.* The children who grow up in the consistently dysfunctional homes are those children who did not receive the affirmations which would help them create the kind of healthy self-esteem which keeps them going—which "fuels the fire" to help them attain the high levels of tenacity and performance these athletes do. Because, *that's what it takes!* Unfortunately, children in our society do not receive *enough* affirmations, they do not receive *enough honest* affirmations, and they do not receive *enough honest and consistent* affirmations. It is our job to change that in our families.

The healthy and positive affirmations that we present to our children typically come in two different packages:

Affirmations for performance
Affirmations for personhood

Both are essential, and a balance between the two is very necessary. We tend to lean much heavier on affirming our children for their performance, because it is their performance which is much more readily noticeable and brought to our attention. From a very early age our children have been coming to us and saying, "See—look what I did." They brought us their scribbles on a piece of paper and told us it was a picture of us. They made a worm with a piece of clay. They picked a flower from the neighbor's garden and brought it to us. They got good grades. They did well in a band concert or athletic event. With our children there has always been an ongoing parade of events and performances for which they looked to us for affirmation, to hear from us, "That's really nice," or, "You did really well!"

It is the affirmations for *personhood* that often go wanting. And these are extremely important because without them, a child learns that their worth is entirely *performance-based* and this can create an endless loop of frustration creating questions that never seem to go away for these children as they grow older:

I wonder *how much is enough?*
What does *good enough* look like?
If I don't keep improving every time, am I *worth less?*

The pure diet of performance-based affirmations can be just as debilitating to a child over time as no affirmations at all. When I work with adults who were affirmed as children primarily for their performance, I find that many of them have an extremely difficult time determining *their own criteria for success* in any endeavor, but especially in their professional lives. They continue to need to hear from outside sources, "You're a good boy (or girl). You've done a good job." And, although we ALL need affirmations, even as adults, for our performance, we must be able to personally determine our criteria for success, and have an inner confidence that indicates our worth beyond what anyone outside may say or think. To achieve this sense in children, that they can then take into adulthood, requires *consistent affirmation that they are valid and valuable human beings on the face of the earth **regardless** of how they perform!*

I remember attempting to explain "cause and effect" to Chloë one morning. The whole family was involved in picking up the house and putting things back where they belonged. The kids had been wanting to go to a little ice cream store near our home, and the deal we made with them was that we would all go get ice cream after the house was picked up. Chloë pitched in and had worked very hard to clean her room, to the best of her four-year-old abilities, and was now eager to get her ice cream. It was time for the object lesson.

"Chloë, do you know *why* daddy is going to take you to get ice cream right now?"

"Uh-huh."

I'm not sure what I was expecting from a four year old in response to that question, but *that wasn't it.* Wanting her to *get it* about cause and effect (didn't we talk about unrealistic expectations and faulty communication just a few chapters ago?), I pursued the issue.

"Chloë, tell daddy *why* I am taking you to get ice cream right now."

Without hesitation she smiled, and answered, *"Because I'm your Princess."* She had me there!

"Princess" has been my pet name for Chloë since she was born. And with each of her passing interests, I have equated her "kingdom" to that subject. When Winnie the Pooh was primary, I would tell her, "Chloë, you are my favorite Pooh Princess of all time." When Pocahontas was the focus, I would tell her, "Chloë, you are my most favorite Pocahontas Princess in the whole world." And when the Hunchback of Notre Dame came out, she would ask, "Daddy, am I your most favorite Esmeralda Princess in the whole world?" "In the whole universe, Chloë," I would assure her. She had gotten used to the princess mode and was more familiar with that than the performance mode.

It is easy to go too far in either direction, and balance becomes necessary, even though it is difficult to achieve. Every now and again, after I've had one of those interactions with Chloë like I described above, Colette will smile and raise the pinky on her hand, the universal signal of, "Boy, does she have *you* wrapped around her little finger!" We don't need to keep score, but we *do* need to be aware that we *are* mixing and matching our performance and personhood affirmations.

Some examples of personhood affirmations are:
"I'm so glad you're my kid."
"I'm so glad God gave you to me to take care of."
"You are very special."
"You are unique in all the world."
"You're a one-of-a-kind special boy (or girl)"
*"I want you to know **I really love you.**"*
"Do you know how special you are?"
"I think you're great!"
"You're my most favorite four year old in the universe."
"You are a very kind girl."
"That was very generous of you."

As we consistently and openly engage in these kinds of behaviors, our children will begin to mimic those behaviors at each stage of their development, using the concepts to which they can relate.

Nicholas was feeling particularly magnanimous one afternoon, and he put his arm around his sister, gave her a hug and said,

"Chloë, I love you all the way to the moon and stars and back again."

Chloë, who was three at the time, considered the compliment momentarily and decided to return the favor.

"Nonnie, I love you all the way to Pizza Hut!"

And while Nicholas felt that he had been a bit shortchanged, Chloë had responded with something that to her was quite extensive and meaningful.

It is also crucial that our performance affirmations be honest assessments of the child's capabilities. Our dishonesty, even though it was intended to build them up and make them feel good more often sets them up for failure and anger when they encounter the real world.

While working in the yard one Saturday morning, I looked up to see a neighbor attempting to teach his five-year-old to ride a two-wheeler bike. Amanda was the youngest in the neighborhood at the time, and none of the other kids still had their training wheels on their bikes, and *she wanted hers off!* The father had obliged her and was now running alongside the bike, his hand grasping the back of the seat to hold the bike upright while his daughter pedaled and steered. And she was having the time of her life. Amanda was squealing and laughing, and all the while he was telling her, "You're doing great! You're a super bike rider. I can't believe you're doing so well. You're going to be racing all the other kids by this afternoon."

All the while, his hand never left the back of her seat.

This went on for about half an hour and the father was now huffing, puffing, and struggling to keep up. During one pass I looked up and said, "You must be exhausted." His response: "I am…but I don't want her to fall."

They disappeared shortly after that. I chuckled, imagining the father collapsed in a lawn chair on the deck with a cold Coke in his hand. About 45 minutes later, I heard a crash and then heard Amanda begin to cry. I didn't even have to look up to know what had happened. She had launched out of her driveway, down the sidewalk, and immediately crashed into the neighbor's hedges. As I ran up the street, and her father ran out of the house, we were relieved to find that she really wasn't hurt. But she was very *angry*. Her first comments to her father were,

"But, you *told* me I was a good bike rider."

"You *told* me I could race the other kids this afternoon."

The father's affirmations had given Amanda a false sense of her capabilities, and had therefore, figuratively and literally, set her up for a fall. It is far better that we give our children honest assessments in our affirmations, and then teach them the processes for improvement, supporting them as they advance.

2. We must teach our children to think, imagine, dream, create, and problem-solve at each level of their development

Leo Buscaglia tells the story of a young man in an elementary art class whose teacher had gone to the blackboard, drawn something that resembled a lollipop, and told the class, "Today we are going to draw trees. Take your crayons and paper, and draw a tree, like I have on the board." This young man decided that what he saw on the board did not look like any tree *he* had ever seen. He took his browns, blacks, greens, reds, yellows, magentas, grays, and went to work. He had branches going in every direction, he had swirls of leaves, he had rugged scribbles of bark and trunk. And he was having a grand time. After the teacher had collected and reviewed the papers, she contacted the school psychologist to set up an evaluation because she was concerned about "brain damage." But, this had nothing to do with brain damage. It had to do with the fact that this child *knew* trees. He had climbed more trees than his teacher would ever see. He had fallen out of trees, he had smelled trees, tasted trees, watched the leaves fall and gently swirl to the ground, had seen trees struck by lightning and branches shattered.

He knew trees!

And he was giving a very accurate depiction of his *experience* with trees.

I'm reminded of an educational program on PBS called *The Magic School Bus,* an animated series with the voice of Lily Tomlin as "Miss Frizzle," the eccentric and creative teacher. Her mandate to the class before every project, endeavor, and adventure:

Take chances!
Make mistakes!
*Get **messy!***

This coincides with the belief of eminent child psychologist Jean Piaget, who wisely observed:

"A child's errors are actually natural steps to understanding."

When we confine our children to rigid, predetermined patterns of thinking we typically do it for two reasons: It's *easier* for us, and it doesn't require us to leave our *comfort zones*. When a child wants to explore, they frequently cannot do that without our assistance. And that takes time, energy, and the willingness to do things that perhaps we aren't comfortable with. This is primarily true because *we* were not given the opportunity to "look through windows" differently than did *our* parents.

All children are born with minds without boundaries and imaginations without fences. It is our task to allow them the freedom to process information without predetermined constraints of familiarity.

We were in the car one afternoon, and our discussion somehow turned to a young lady Nathan was dating at the time. Nicholas, who was four at the time, had met this young lady and her sister, but couldn't remember the sister's name. "What is Nancy's sister's name," he asked. None of us could remember. "If we can't remember her real name, I guess we'll have to make one up so we know who we're talking about."

"Okay, Nicholas, what name would you like to give her?"

"Hmmm... I think I'll name her Pediatric AIDS Foundation."

We were aghast! We had no idea where he had heard about PAF, but he apparently had from somewhere, and as he processed the information, he created an opportunity to present something from his own, unique perspective. We did tell him, however, that it probably would be a good idea to *find out* what her name was and call her by her name, because names were very important things and we each had our own special one. He agreed, and we went on from there.

Teaching our children to think and to problem-solve is often difficult for us as adults because, again, it is easier to just do it for them, give them the answer, so that *we* can get on with life in our own way. And in doing so, we deprive them of an opportunity to grow.

One of the staff psychiatrists to whom I reported when I was in the military was a short, intense doctor from the East Coast. There was a technique he used in doing supervision that I have found to be extremely helpful, educational, and instructive not only with the interns I supervise, but also with my children.

When we went to his office to present a case, or request medications for a patient, there was a clear mandate that we had better come prepared. We had to have a complete history, a diagnosis, a treatment plan, and suggestions for medications including types, brands, and dosages. If at any point he asked a question for which we didn't have an answer, there was a good chance we would be told to leave and not come back until we were prepared. "Don't bring me a problem unless you also bring two possible solutions," he yelled down the hallway after he had tersely dismissed me from his office one morning. It was not that he was wanting us to do his job or to be experts in the field of psychopharmacology or psychopathology. He only wanted to know that we had thought the *process through and had attempted to assess the situation fully before we had brought it to him!* We didn't have to be right or have all the answers. When we presented our plans, he always took an extensive amount of time going over them with us, challenging us to look at things just a little bit differently, or suggesting why a different medication or approach might work better, and why. He used every experience as an opportunity for us to think and to learn.

Shortly after Nathan turned 16, he decided, like most 16-year-old boys, that he *had* to have a car. He was working after school and on weekends, and felt that he could pull it off. However, he had failed to define "pull it off" for me.

"Dad, I've been thinking. I really think that I should get a car. Then I wouldn't have to use yours or Mom's. I'm sure you can see the benefit in that."

"Okay, Nate, what's your plan?"

"My plan…?"

"Yes, tell me how you're going to pull this off. I need a plan that tells me how you're going to look for a car, decide which one is right for you, determine how much you can pay, figure out how much you think it will cost you to maintain it, prices for insurance… a plan."

"Oh… a plan… I guess I don't have one right now."

I asked Nate to come back to me with a plan and proposal for getting his own car. And, a week later he did! There were still some kinks in it, but, I had told him that the plan didn't have to be perfect or even have all of the right ingredients. I only wanted to know that he had thought it through and attempted to solve the problems involved.

This is important even with smaller children. At each stage of development a child already has problem-solving skills to help them through that stage. The hot stove example is a good one. It doesn't take the small child very long to learn that the hot stove will cause pain and that they need to stay away from it. Unfortunately, the small child does not possess the cognitive skills to hear from a parent, "don't touch the stove or you'll be burned," without having to experience it on his own. With children four and five years old, it is *not* too early to help them get into the habit of personal, creative problem solving. If the child comes to you with an issue or difficulty, it is first important that you *listen* to the child to fully understand what the issue is *for them*. Then, before you problem-solve for them, ask the questions:

*How do **you** think we should handle this?*
*What do **you** think we should do?*

And then help them evaluate the answers they have given you. Walk them through the pros and cons of their answers. Help them to look at the issue just a little bit differently, like, "Well, what do you think would happen if we did this…?" And through this process, guide them to come up with the answer that will be best for them and the situation. An additional reason that this is so beneficial to you and the child is that if the child comes up with the answer, even through your guidance, they have a far greater tendency to "own" that answer and follow through behaviorally. It is far more difficult to dismiss the answer as simply "something my parent told me to do."

3. Present opportunities to challenge and push the limits

It is generally from a position of laziness, naïveté or arrogance that any parent believes that they can personally provide their children with everything they need. Realistically, we each come from personal *worlds* so small that to *confine* a child to that world and deprive them of an opportunity to expand and grow beyond the *comfortable* worlds we have created for ourselves is tantamount to child abuse!

It is just as negligent to believe that when we *turn our children over* to the school system, they are going to receive the *total* education that will prepare them to be healthy individuals in the world.

It is a primary task of healthy parents to actively pursue and present opportunities to our children to experience as much of the world as is theirs to experience.

One of the easiest (that is, most user-friendly to parents) *and* most beneficial ways to open up our children to the *possibilities* is through *reading*. When parents ask what skills they should put major attention and focus on for their children, my answer is always the same—"Teach them to read as early as possible. Spend time reading *to* them and *with* them. Provide a wide variety of things for them to read. Enroll them in summer reading programs and take them to the library on a regular basis. Help them read, read, read! Reading helps them explore the world. They can visit exotic places and can do fun, challenging, and even dangerous things through reading. Reading opens up the *differences* in the world and helps prepare a child to accept those differences. There is *nowhere* a child cannot go through reading. Reading also opens up the possibilities for what the child might like to do, both short- and long-term.

Reading a book about Joe Namath or Arthur Ashe can encourage a young person to explore football or tennis in their communities. Many a young girl has been inspired by a book on Madame Curie to pursue the sciences. A simple book on Egypt or mummies can be instrumental in helping a child develop an interest in archaeology, travel, the sciences, or simply rock collecting. The child has the opportunity to develop an "I can" attitude—"If *they* can do it, so can I"—as they explore the possibilities presented to them.

It is then up to us to present experiential opportunities in order for the children to touch the possibilities. Trips to the museum, library, rock quarry, arts and crafts fair, fire or police station, community swimming pool or tennis courts all facilitate the conscious awareness of the child to the enormous possibilities.

Of course, if we were to undertake the task alone we would be overwhelmed because it is more than a full time job to accomplish. We must use all of the resources available to assist us in this process. Organizations like Scouting, community swim and tennis teams, parks and recreation programs like Little League baseball and peewee football, educational programs offered by schools, colleges, and libraries are typically available in every community at minimal cost. Some even offer financial assistance and scholarships to families in need. The resources are there. We should take advantage of them.

Lastly, we must then *actively support our children as they experience their endeavor.* This means much more than transporting them to and fro (or getting them to the car pool on time). It means talking to them about what they're doing. It requires taking the time to let them know what they are doing is important to you and that you are really interested in their thoughts and feelings. It requires helping them problem-solve when they run into a problem, as well as letting them be responsible and accountable for the consequences of their decisions and behaviors.

In these ways we can enhance every experience for our children and give them the support and courage to pursue many other opportunities, creating well-rounded, interesting, interested, and healthy children.

4. We must create a safe, accepting place for our children to express their fears and emotions

Like most children, mine were afraid of thunder and lightning when they were young. The combinations of bright light and noise would wake them from a sound sleep and they would bound from their bedrooms into ours, often in tears.

"I'm scared," they would say. And for the longest time I replied, "It's only light and noise, it's outside, and it can't hurt you. Now, go back to bed." And they would, until the next bolt of lightning came along. After one particularly stormy (and sleepless) night, I commented to Colette that "although they're getting older, they don't seem to be getting over their fears of storms." Her reply both surprised and provoked me to think about the issue from another perspective.

"Maybe it's because you don't allow them to *have* their fears. You're always telling them that there's nothing to be afraid of, and discounting the fact that, for *them,* there *is* something to be afraid of. Perhaps you should try *acknowledging their fears and letting them know that it's okay to be afraid.*"

That was a tremendous revelation for me. I was considering their fears from the viewpoint of who I was. Not from the viewpoint of who they were. From that point on, when the thunder and lightning struck and they bounded into our room, the responses to their fears were, "Yeah, that was *really loud,* wasn't it? Wow, that was the biggest thunder-boomer I ever heard," and we allowed them to snuggle with us for a few minutes until things calmed down. On one occasion, we all got out of bed, went into the living room, and watched through the windows as a storm moved toward us across Lake Michigan. The children sat on our laps and watched in awe as the lightning strikes flashed out over the lake. We would count the seconds before we heard the thunder. In this way we were able to help them *confront* their fears, and not have to deny them. At the same time we were able to teach them the beauty, majesty, and power of God over our earth. Then, when it was all over, they would go back to their beds. As we continued this process, their midnight sojourns into our bedroom during storms became less and less, and I learned a valuable lesson about acceptance.

The primary task in accepting our children's emotions, regardless of what they are, is to *listen* to what the experience that triggered the emotions is like for the child. If they are *afraid,* listen to the experience of what made them fearful. If they are *angry,* listen to the experience that made them angry, non-judgmentally, listening to get information to help you understand—not deny, take away, justify, or criticize.

The secondary task in helping our children deal with the emotion is to help them separate *feeling from thought from behavior.* In doing this, we teach our children that "just because we felt *anger,* and *thought* about punching our sister in the nose, we didn't have to *act* on that feeling and thought, and actually punch her in the nose, which would have resulted in *consequences* that we might not want to go through."

In *no* way do we want to deprive the child of the *feeling* or the *thought.* After all, we can't even achieve that as adults. What we do want to achieve is teaching them that they have the power and control to not *act* on the feelings and thoughts if it is not the healthy thing to do. In our family we have many dialogues about *choices*. We refer to our children's behaviors in terms of *good choices* and *bad choices*. This allows them to realize that the choices they make are just that—*their choices,* and that we will expect them to be responsible for the consequences of those choices.

We then have to teach them how to establish clear and healthy boundaries regarding appropriate and inappropriate ways to act out our thoughts and feelings. *We must remember that the boundaries that our children will adhere to have nothing to do with what we **tell** them and everything to do with what we **show** them.* They will only observe the boundaries that are set up and adhered to within the family system. If we tell them, "no hitting," but the family system boundary permits hitting among adults, or adults to children, then the verbal rule of "no hitting" is irrelevant to them.

Providing for our children a safe place within which to have and express emotions, and teaching them healthy ways to manifest those emotions, is a primary factor in creating healthy children for the future.

5. We must teach our children to accept ambiguity and differences

In our human nature, the greatest roadblock to the acceptance of ambiguity and differences is *fear.* H.A. Overstreet once made the statement, "To hate and to fear is to be psychologically ill...it is, in fact, the consuming illness of our time." Both hatred and fear, in regard to ambiguity and differences, are bred by the anxiety we experience when we encounter *something we don't understand.* In our lack of understanding, and in an attempt to reduce our anxiety, we have a propensity to reject or deny whatever the object of our ignorance is. The narrower our focus, the more rigid our stance, and more opportunity for the rejection of differences is present. There are numerous examples throughout the world of havoc created by the lack of acceptance of differences. In our own country there continues to be rampant racism. In my sleepy little community, a cross was burned on the lawn of an African-American pastor, the only family of color in our neighborhood. Black churches are being burned down in frightening numbers. Religious bias, cultural bias, financial and social snobbery, gender bias, sexual preference bias—all are alarmingly alive and well throughout every community in every state across our nation—across our world. And the primary perpetrators of these ignorant transactions are the children who learned from their parents who learned from their parents that "different was bad."

Our task as parents in this regard is to educate our children concerning differences in a more factual and less emotional and judgmental way. It is not necessary to criticize a practicing Jew. It IS necessary to learn about Judaism, where it comes from, what it's foundation is, what the difference is between Jewish nationalism—called Zionism—and the Jewish religion. In teaching our children about differences, they become far less foreboding and anxiety producing. In removing the critical judgment of those things we don't understand, we can teach our children that not everything comes down to an issue of right and wrong. They can *appreciate* the differences in people without compromising or denying that which is important to them. It is in the *education* that the acceptance occurs. And if we, as parents, can educate ourselves to reduce *our* fears regarding differences, our children will be much more tolerant and accepting as they grow and know.

6. We must prepare our children to leave home with an accurate assessment of how the "real world" works

One of the primary tasks of parenting is to protect our children from pain. We do this in a variety of ways. Sometimes we don't allow them to be in the position to get hurt. We tell them, "No, you can't cross the street by yourself. You might get hurt." Or that they can't go to the store alone, or to the restroom in the mall alone, or to the party, or to the dance, or camping.

Other times we attempt to protect them by structuring the situation in such a way as to minimize their opportunity to get hurt. "Okay, you can play outside after dinner, but don't go off the block, and you must come home when the streetlights come on." Or, "You can go to the dance, but I will take you and pick you up at 10 o'clock. And I'm going to call the school to make sure there will be chaperones." If the boundaries are rigid and unreasonable in regard to the child's developmental status, or created chiefly to diminish the parent's anxiety (as opposed to being in the best interest of the child), that child will feel smothered, controlled, untrustworthy, and have a sense that they have diminished worth or value to the family. Ultimately, that child will be required to misbehave and act out inappropriately in an effort to break free from the strangulation of the rigidity and be able to leave the family. Often the "leaving" comes in the form of being "ejected" as a result of the parents inability to handle the acting-out behaviors.

It is the negligent parent who *neither* creates nor maintains boundaries.

A child, under those circumstances, feels abandoned, neglected, and of diminished worth and value to the family. The child may think, "I don't want them to control me, but if they tried to control me, then I would have a sense that I was of some importance to them." This child also will be required to misbehave and act out inappropriately. But the reason is entirely different—it is to be noticed and acknowledged, and to force the parents to create some boundaries that the child can react to. The message to the parents is, "Let me know how far I can go here. I may try to push and exceed the boundaries, but at least I have to have something to react to."

Creating a balance between those two positions is a difficult and dynamic task. It changes on an ongoing basis along with the child's development, personality, capabilities and limitations, and life experiences. And it is impossible under the best of circumstances for a parent to keep up with all of those changes. How, then, are we ever going to be able to prepare our children to leave home and take care of themselves? Once again, the answer lies in a process that is readily available to us in a myriad of shapes and sizes:

Education: Often we, as parents, are reluctant to expose our children to the "world" because it is not a friendly place much of the time. There is death, disease, pornography, sex, addiction, perversion, malice, greed— all of those things "out there," and we don't want our children to see or experience it. The fact of the matter is that, much of the time, *we* don't want to be exposed to it or have to deal with it. So, in our own denial we deprive our children of an opportunity to learn *how* to deal with what the world has in store for them.

Another inappropriate way that parents tend to deal with "real world" issues is by taking the position, "I don't have to expose them to it. They'll be exposed to it soon enough."

Probably sooner than you think…

An informal survey in a community near our home indicated that among school-age children who were involved sexually, from petting to fondling to intercourse, the average beginning age was 13 years old. And, yet, I hear from parents that they don't want to talk to their children about sex, or condoms, or birth control, or AIDS because "it might put ideas in their heads that weren't there before." Believe me, the ideas *are* there. Just because you haven't seen visible proof of acting-out behaviors does not mean they don't exist, or at least are not present in the thought process implanted by peer pressure, the media, or simple curiosity.

"Most parents don't worry about a daughter until she fails to show up for breakfast. Then it is too late," says author Frank McKinney Hubbard.

He continues, "Only a mother would think her daughter has been a good girl when she returns from a date with a Gideon Bible in her handbag." It's a humorous observation on the surface, but a frightening commentary considering the continued climb of sexually transmitted diseases in not just our states and cities, but just down the street as well.

What are the major areas about which we need to make sure our children have the correct information as they grow up in our homes? Let's examine a few.

Sex: We need to ensure that our children have the latest information in birth control, reproductive systems, sexually transmitted diseases, sexual hygiene, peer pressure, myths perpetuated by the media regarding sexuality, and the moral/spiritual/ethical values we adhere to as a family. We need to have the *correct* information available for them, from reliable sources, and we need to discuss the information with them, not just give them the information and say, "Here, read this. It's some stuff you need to know." We have to be willing to push ourselves out of our comfort zones to discuss material that we may feel uneasy discussing or thinking about.

When do we discuss these things with our children? Certainly not at one sitting, and not at the same time for all children. As you *listen* to your children, and hear what concerns them, or what is piquing their interests, you will have a sense of how much material to share with them at any given point in time. If you're not sure, test the waters. Start with something small. One of three things is going to happen. They may express a great deal of interest and that is an indicator for you to go on. The may express discomfort or uneasiness. It then becomes important to discuss the discomfort and prepare the child to talk about it another time. Or, they may be bored and disinterested in what you have to say. This is an indicator that they are probably not ready to talk about the issue, and it should be brought up at a later date.

Do not wait for the child to come to you with the issue—it is *your* obligation to go to them.

Religion: It is important to educate our children not only about the religion you personally adhere to, but about the varieties of religions throughout the world. It is also important that you teach them the history of your faith, where it came from, what it split from, and most importantly, what it means to *you*, and why you believe in it. The child needs to be taught to compare and contrast, to make intelligent decisions about religious philosophies, and to *question*. It is the questioning part that frightens most parents and prevents them from making the choice to either educate or allow their children to explore the backgrounds of other faiths. The fear is that if the child is exposed to other religions, then the family faith will no longer *hold them*. My response to that dilemma is to acknowledge that that option is available regardless of whether or not the parent participates in an educational and investigative process towards religion. My experience has been that a child will tend to gravitate toward what they see consistently working in the lives of the parents. *Don't ever underestimate the power of the family system in the lives of the children.* If those parents *live* their faith, and the child experiences the results of their life of faith as individuals and as a family, then the investigation of other faiths will have the tendency to only build an acceptance of differences, not lure the child away.

Politics: There are very few young people who would disagree that we have a great country. Unfortunately, a majority of them have absolutely no idea of how it really works. Schools offer some opportunities to educate our children in regard to politics, but as parents we should have "dinner table discussions" of what is going on politically in our country. If we're Republican, Democrat, Independent, or adhere to some other political belief, we need to be able to share with our children the dynamics behind our choices. What makes one party or one candidate different from the other? What does the House or Senate do? Where do Special Prosecutors come from? The newspaper is a good source of information regarding what is happening politically, and visits to the nation's capital, state capitals, and city hall are beneficial in teaching our children about the political history of our country. Attendance at a town meeting or city council meeting can allow a child to experience the political mechanism in action. Many homes have computers and on-line services with vast amounts of information just the "click" of a button away.

Our children are going to be running this country in the next 40 years. We owe it to them to give them a glimpse of how it works!

Money: At no time in history is more money that we *don't have* being spent on more things we *don't really need*. Credit card debt is at an all-time high. We have found that there are literally thousands of lending sources just waiting to accommodate our need to have more and more money, and that we most often have the money spent on speculation before it ever reaches our pockets. One of the ramifications of a generally nonchalant attitude toward money is that we have provided far more for our children than they know how to handle, and many of them have adopted an attitude of *entitlement,* which manifests itself as, "No matter, my folks will buy it for me," or, "It doesn't matter if I don't take care of it, or if it breaks. My parents will get me another one." Rather than doing battle with the 14-year-old who says, "I won't wear those discount store jeans," we buy instead the $60 designer jeans that end up in a heap on the floor in the corner of the bedroom. We haven't done a very good job, in many cases, educating our children about money. Nor have we presented them with adequate opportunities to work for it. Several options in educating our children about money are:

1. At a very early age, present them opportunities to earn money. This will usually come from doing small jobs around the house. It is important, however, to distinguish between those tasks that we do in our families simply by virtue of the fact that we are a participating family member, and those tasks which are over and above, for which we can compensate the child. There is little more irritating than the child, when asked to help around the house, who replies, "What are you going to give me for it?"

2. Start a savings account at the bank. I happened to overhear Nicholas telling his mother that he had saved over $100 in the bank in his "Space Camp" fund. I was astounded, because I also knew that his piggy bank was full of money he had received through birthdays, allowance, and some extra chores around the house. He had his deposit book, and was checking in on his progress. He felt good, because he had a goal and he could see the strides he was making toward that goal.

3. Teach children how much things cost. Take them shopping with you, and let them help "cost compare," seeing which item is the better value, and what is on sale .

4. Teach them about return on investment. With their $6 they would be able to: a.) go to a matinee movie with a friend, complete with popcorn; b.) buy four packages of baseball cards; or, c.) save it until it reaches $18 and go to the church youth retreat with the other $18 that mom and dad said they would chip in. Teaching the child to evaluate their return on investment enables them to curb the emotional impulse-buying that always leaves them broke.

Addiction: I regard addiction as the biggest threat to family stability in our country today. Drug and alcohol abuse is destroying homes and lives at an increasingly alarming rate. Addiction is at the root of many financial, marital, familial, and social problems. Alcohol and drugs are readily available to children of all ages at any time. Several years ago I sat with a city council member in the back of a shopping center parking lot on a Saturday evening and watched a steady stream of underage adolescents either buying the alcohol directly or paying someone else to go in and get it for them. At the age of 6, Nathan came home from school with a joint and said, "Hey, Dad, look what some kid at school gave me." In my clinical practice, I received a call from a fifth-grade teacher who, concerned over a female student with a chronic cough, confiscated the cough syrup bottle to find it filled with straight vodka.

We need to educate our children that addiction has no regard for person, age, sex, or status. It is a disease beyond the control of those individuals who experience it. Homes, relationships, and even lives can be destroyed by the power of addiction.

1. Share stories with them of famous people who have struggled with addiction, like Betty Ford, and others.

2. Get the correct information about the effects of drugs and alcohol and discuss the information with them.

3. Make sure *you* are informed about the signs and symptoms of substance abuse.

4. Educate your children about the methods of dealing with peer pressure.

5. Make it easy for them to talk to you about what is happening around them in regard to drugs and alcohol by offering to listen, then listening, then offering input, and giving the input in a supportive way rather than a critical way. Statements like, "That must really be tough for you when your friends are drinking. How do you handle it?" will gain far more ground than statements like, "Well, you know you better not hang around with those kids anymore, or you'll turn out just like them. Get rid of them. You can always find other friends who don't do that kind of stuff."

6. At the first sign of any difficulty in the area of substance abuse, get professional help immediately. All too often after a drug overdose, I've heard parents say, "I knew they were using but I didn't know it was this bad," or, "I knew they were using, but I thought it was just a passing thing and that we could handle it at home. I never thought it would come to this." Because this is such a widespread problem in every community, resources abound with which you can get prompt attention and assistance.

A phrase that keeps echoing throughout our society is, *Children are our future.* Another is, *Children are our best natural resource.* Yet another is, *Chil-*

dren are the hope of things to come. I would like to leave you with these thoughts. Children are our shadows and our mirrors. They follow us and they reflect us. On them we project all that we are and all that we need. On us they project all that we have taught them to be. They are our responsibility, and they challenge our irresponsibility.

Every child is destined for greatness.

As we are able to separate them from ourselves, and help them determine who God created them to be, with all of their unique characteristics, gifts, talents, limitations, and capabilities, we will be able to participate *in the hope, and the light, and the glory that is our children.*

Shadowchaser

TURN BACK TO THE BIAS-R AT THE END OF CHAPTER 3. CHOOSE THREE ISSUES THAT YOU GIVE SIGNIFICANT IMPORTANCE TO AND ASK YOUR CHILDREN, "WHAT IS THE MESSAGE THAT I AM SENDING YOU ABOUT THIS ISSUE?" DID THEIR ANSWERS SURPRISE YOU? WHICH ONES, AND FOR WHAT REASONS? NOW CONSIDER THE FOLLOWING QUESTIONS:

HOW DO YOU DISCIPLINE YOUR CHILDREN?

WHAT ARE YOU TRYING TO ACCOMPLISH THROUGH YOUR DISCIPLINE?

WHAT DO YOU BELIEVE YOU ARE TEACHING YOUR CHILDREN THROUGH THE WAY YOU DISCIPLINE THEM?

HOW HAVE YOU TAUGHT YOUR CHILDREN TO MAKE DECISIONS?

HOW IS YOUR STANDARD OF MORAL INTEGRITY REFLECTED IN YOUR CHILDREN?

HOW ARE YOUR SPIRITUAL VALUES REFLECTED IN YOUR CHILDREN?

IN WHAT AREAS DO YOU NEED TO IMPROVE YOUR OWN EXAMPLE IN ORDER FOR YOUR CHILDREN TO HAVE A HEALTHY ROLE MODEL FOR GROWTH?

DANCING WITH YESTERDAY'S SHADOWS

Epilogue

*"Do not conform any longer
to the pattern of this world,
but be transformed by the renewing of your mind.
Then you will be able to test and approve
what God's will is—
his good, pleasing, and perfect will."*
–Romans 12:2

*"When I am grown to man's estate
I shall be very proud and great,
And tell the other girls and boys
Not to meddle with my toys."*
–Robert Louis Stevenson

*"The purpose of learning is to grow,
and our minds,
unlike our bodies,
can continue growing
as we continue to live."*
–Mortimer Adler

There is a story of two hunters who, while walking through the woods looking for deer, stumbled across an old farmyard. At first glance, the two thought it was deserted. There were old car parts and tractor pieces lying about. The barn was in great disrepair, the fences needed mending, and the house was little more than a shack. The only evidence that it was still a working farm were the few chickens and a goat wandering about nearby. As they continued walking they came to a well near the middle of the property. Looking down the old well they noticed that they couldn't see the bottom, and this started a conversation about just how deep that old well might be.

"I reckon there's only one way to find out how deep this well is," said the one hunter. "We'll throw something down it, and then we'll listen for the splash."

"Good idea," replied the other, "What shall we send down the shaft?"

They looked around them, and the closest thing they saw was an old transmission lying on the ground nearby. Both men lifted the transmission over the edge of the well, dropped it, and listened.

Although it was only a matter of seconds, it seemed like a long time to the men until they heard the "sploosh" of the transmission hitting the water below.

"That certainly is a *deep* one," commented one of the hunters.

"Sure is," replied the other.

As they turned to leave, the men were suddenly confronted with the goat they had seen earlier. The goat was charging right at them! Its head was down and it was running so fast that its feet barely touched the ground. At the last possible moment both men jumped aside, and the goat charged right past them, bleating loudly, and fell straight down the well!

The men stared at each other. Then at the well. Then at each other again. They had never seen anything like that before in their lives. They walked away from the well, shaking their heads in amazement at what they had just witnessed. They hadn't gone very far when they were approached by the farmer who owned the property. They chatted for a time, and the farmer gave them permission to hunt on his property. As they were about to leave the farmer asked, "By the way, have either of you fellows seen my goat?"

"Have we seen your *goat?!* Your fool goat tried to kill us. He charged at us and we barely had time to jump aside before he hit us. Luckily he missed—but he was going so fast that he ran right into the old well. That was a *crazy* old goat. You should have had him tied up."

The farmer scratched his head and looked around him. "I thought I did have him tied up. In fact, I'm *sure* I had him tied up. I tied him to an old transmission."

The moral of the story is a simple, yet profound one:

You will follow what you're tied to!

This book has been all about what you're tied to and how that impacts you, your marriage, your families—every aspect of your life, every day of your life. The design was intended to challenge you to a time of introspection regarding

who you are,
where you come from
and,
what you bring with you into your relationships.

The intent was to get you to look into the mirror of your being to figure out what messages you had received, internalized, and by which you operated your life, whether out of habit, unconscious loyalty, or because they truly fit who you were and who you desired to be.

Having read this book, you now know too much to ever look at your life in quite the same way again. You will be required to examine much more closely your part in relationships, and have the exciting opportunity to help those relationships prosper and grow in ways that were never before possible.

You now have an opportunity to remove yourself from the shadows, acknowledging and celebrating who you are, and who you *choose to be.* Not everyone around you will understand or accept this new-found faith in your personhood. During a recent television episode of *"Star Trek,"* a Bajoran Major was attempting to explain to a Changeling the finer aspects of the Bajoran religion. Her response to his confusion and skepticism was classic.

*"It's a **faith thing.** If you don't have it, you can't understand it. If you have it— no explanation is necessary."*

And so, this book is completed—but the journey for some has just begun. For them this will have been new information, necessary to digest and contemplate, to try on tentatively like one might experiment with a new style of clothes, and to nervously attempt to break out of old patterns. For them there will be a certain degree of anxiety and fear.

"What if these principles don't apply to me?"
"What if my friends and family won't like me anymore?"
"What if the emotional price is too high?"
"What if I don't know how to do it 'right'?"
"What might I lose—or gain—in the process?"
"What if I could be free of the dance?"
"I think I'll try it—little by little—but I'm really scared!"
*"Okay, it's time—ready... set... **go!**"*

For those individuals I say— It's okay to be tentative, okay to be scared, and okay to take it slow—after all, you have the rest of your life. Test the waters with your toes. As you do, I believe you'll want to jump in—because the water is fine.

For others, this book was a diversion while they contemplated all of the good and viable reasons the tasks contained within presented too formidable a challenge to attempt. For them, the shadows will remain and the dance will continue. They will periodically complain that "it isn't fair and it isn't my fault," but their comfort in the chaos will keep them bound there.

And for the rest, it will become a stepping stone to continued growth and a journey toward health and fulfillment begun some time ago. They have said goodbye to the shadows before. Perhaps more than once. And they have stopped dancing for the most part, although at times it is difficult to resist the urge. It's okay to notice the urge. It's *normal* to feel the urge. You no longer feel the need to *act on* that urge—but it will occasionally present itself.

With these individuals there is a contentment that comes with the understanding and acceptance that the journey has no end in this lifetime, that the process will continue as long as life itself continues. Also, with these individuals, there is an excitement that accompanies the knowledge and experience that they are free to dance a new dance, to sing, to dream, to have vision, to create, to take chances, make mistakes and get messy, and above all else—

to impart upon their children these same opportunities
to be different, and unique, and wonderful—
to be themselves!

This book is an invitation to remove the armor of loyalty that has kept us bound in our personal dysfunctional behaviors.

It is an invitation to shed the garment of fear that has prevented us from accepting all the wonderment that life has to offer—all of the good, all of the bad, all of the differences, all of the things we cannot understand, and all of the things we would rather not look at.

It is an invitation to remove the chains of unhealthy homeostasis in order to be able to *move about freely* into new realms of behavior and new patterns of thinking. It also is an invitation to use our new-found abilities to reject those connections that preserved an unhealthy family system at the expense of our personhood and well-being.

Martin Buber, in his book, *Between Man and Man*, writes, "Each of us is encased in an armor whose task is to ward off signs. Signs happen to us without respite, living means being addressed, we would need only to present ourselves and perceive. But the risk is too dangerous for us, the soundless thunderings seem to threaten us with annihilation, and from generation to generation we perfect the defense apparatus. All our knowledge assures us,

> "Be calm, everything happens as it must happen, but nothing is directed at you, you are not meant; it is just the world, you can experience it as you like... What occurs to me addresses me."

Just as Buber addresses *the world,* those same concepts apply to the family system. We have defended so heavily in our lives a system which we believed sustained us. At the same time it may have been destroying who we were, who we inwardly desired to be, all of the fantastic possibilities that were before us, and all of the miracle we were capable of becoming. And each of us, wrapped in our loyalty, believed through ignorance that *it was all going to be okay,* because, after all, this was our family. What on earth could be unhealthy about that?

Above all else, this is a *spiritual journey.* Without the sustaining grace and guidance of a compassionate and loving Father God, we will not have the strength or courage to complete the journey. As a result of our impaired relationships with our earthly families, it is often too big a stretch to imagine that our heavenly Father could offer us anything other than the pain and disappointment we've already encountered in our lives. Romans 5:1-2 tells us,

> "By entering through faith into what God has always wanted to do for us—set us right for him, make us fit for him—we have it all together with God because of our Master Jesus." –The Message

The process for the God-connection is the same as the other growth processes we've examined in this book. Look inside yourself—examine the spiritual parts of you, the hurts, pains, miracles, answered prayers—all of it. And then talk with God! Just like you would with a good friend, a healthy parent, a loved and respected teacher. This, too, can be intimidating and frightening as we begin communicating with God on a consistently open and honest level. But, God will listen—and answer.

It is time to approach growth, health, vision, creativity, passion and life with a renewed sense of empowerment. Having the tools and developing the insights will allow you to approach your personhood and your relationships in a new and exciting way. As Henry Ford once said,

"If you think you can,
or you think you can't,
you're absolutely right!"

And finally, for our children's sake, it is my hope and prayer that you will actively give them permission to *fly*—first in their family rooms, then in the backyard, and finally, in the world. Empower them to become all that is possible for them. Support them as they stumble through discovery. Hold them lovingly accountable for the natural consequences of their decisions and behaviors, and, most of all, set the example of freedom from the dance for them.

Look around you...

The shadows are gone...

Bon voyage.